THE ULTIMATE
HERO'S JOURNEY

195 Essential Plot Stages Found in the Best Novels & Movies

Copyright © 2017 by Neal Soloponte
All rights reserved.

No part of this publication may be reproduced, distributed, or transmitted in any form or by any means, including photocopying, recording, or other electronic or mechanical methods, without the prior written permission of the publisher, except in the case of brief quotations embodied in critical reviews and certain other noncommercial uses permitted by copyright law.
All
For permission requests, write to the publisher via email to info@tb-books.com.

Printed in the United States of America

ISBN 978-1548628246

This book may contain copyrighted material the use of which has not always been specifically authorized by the copyright owner. It is being made available in an effort to advance the understanding of works of literature. It is believed that this constitutes a 'fair use' of any such copyrighted material as provided for in section 107 of the US Copyright Law. If you wish to use copyrighted material from this site for purposes of your own that go beyond 'fair use', you must obtain permission from the copyright owner.

TANGO&BLUM
Publishers

Visit us:
www.TB-books.com

Dedicated to Silvana, my sister, who traveled to the end of the world in order to take the first steps into her own Heroine's Journey.

Contents

(Very Short) Introduction v
    Why 195 stages? Why not 196? vii
    A World in four acts viii
    Stages versus scenes ix
    Clichés are the enemy ix
    Types of stages x
    How to use The Ultimate Hero's Journey xii
    Spoiler alert xii
    Last but not least xiii

The Ultimate Hero's Journey:

0 - Hook	Stage 1	1
1 - Setup	Stages 2 to 63	2
2.1 - Reaction	Stages 64 to 118	64
2.2 - Epiphany	Stage 119	119
2.3 - Proaction	Stages 120 to 142	120
3 - Climax	Stages 143 to 185	143
4 - Dénouement	Stages 186 to 195	186

Farewell 196
Index of stages 198

(Very Short) Introduction

What do Harry Potter, The Matrix, Star Wars, and hundreds of other famous stories have in common?

Consider the figure below (it has been going around the web, blogged and reblogged so many times that I couldn't find the source anymore):

> *Harry Potter and the Sorcerer's Stone*
> ~~Star Wars - A New Hope (Synopsis)~~
>
> Harry Potter / ~~Luke Skywalker~~ is an orphan living with his uncle and aunt on the remote wilderness of ~~Tatooine~~ / suburbia. He is rescued from ~~aliens~~ / muggles by wise, bearded ~~Ben Kenobi~~ / Hagrid, who turns out to be a ~~Jedi Knight~~ / Wizard.
>
> Hagrid / ~~Ben~~ reveals to ~~Luke~~ / Harry that ~~Luke's~~ / Harry's father was also a ~~Jedi Knight~~ / wizard, and was the best ~~pilot~~ / Quidditch player he had ever seen.
>
> Harry / ~~Luke~~ is instructed on how to use ~~the lightsaber~~ / a magic wand as he too trains to become a ~~Jedi~~ / wizard.
>
> Harry / ~~Luke~~ has many adventures in ~~the galaxy~~ / Hogwarts and makes new friends like ~~Han Solo and princess Leia~~ / Ron Hermione.
>
> In the course of these adventures he distinguishes himself as a top ~~pilot~~ / Quidditch seeker in the ~~battle of the Death Star~~ / Quidditch match, making the ~~direct hit~~ / catch that secures the ~~Rebel Victory~~ / Gryffindor against the forces of ~~evil~~ / Slytherin.
>
> Luke also sees off the threat of ~~Darth Vader~~ / Lord Voldemort, who we know murdered his ~~uncle and aunt~~ / parents.
>
> In the finale, ~~Luke~~ / Harry and his new friends ~~receive medals of honor~~ / win the House Cup.
>
> All this will be set to an orchestral score by John Williams.

The comparison was surely intended just as a funny observation, (I particularly liked the part about the John William's orchestral score), but it refers to a well established fact: Deep down, all stories are the same. Or at least, they mirror a general, archetypical story, called the **Hero's Journey**, which can be represented like this:

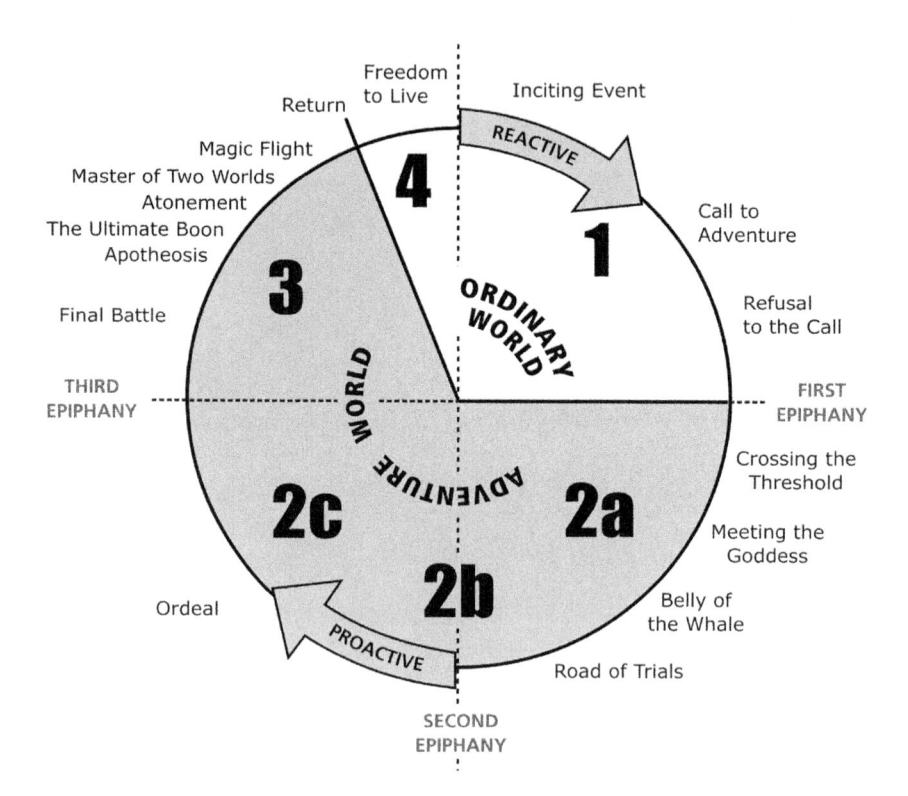

I know that my work here is not original; in fact, I honor the work of scholars like Joseph Campbell and Vladimir Propp, who discovered that most—if not all—works of literature, myths, folkloric tales, and religious texts follow a common narrative structure. But this book intends to be much more detailed and focused than the sources I have consulted with: I present the milestones of the Hero's Journey not just in twelve, fifteen, or seventeen, but in 195 stages. Plus, I include mythical and psychological associations, practical advice for writers, and examples from famous works of fiction.

Why 195 stages? Why not 196?

If the Hero's Journey is described in too few steps—like in the circular graphic in the opposing page—it fails to reflect the parallels between different stories in a useful level of detail. For a critic or a writer, a dozen or so stages fall way too short.

On the other extreme, if you atomize the steps too much (I have seen versions with literally *thousands* of stages), it all becomes very repetitive and blurry. You end up with too many stages that apply to some stories but not to others, which means that many of those stages are not truly fundamental.

So, why 195?

Because that's the number I came to after distilling the essential stages that describe the mythical Hero's Journey as presented in modern bestsellers and blockbusters. Decoding that particular set of steps will inspire us to understand, create, plot, and write stories on a whole new level.

Are all the 195 stages always there?

I am confident in saying that at least eighty percent of them are always there. The sequence changes, the characters change, the symbolism changes, but the stages are there. In fact, stories that leave too many stages out will probably feel hollow and incomplete, because they will not fully resonate with the mythical structure that we have engrained in our minds.

If you are a writer (or aspiring writer), I encourage you to include as many of these stages as possible in your story, even if some stages are represented by just one sentence. The exception would be those stages that only present backstory. *The Matrix,* for example, doesn't deal with Neo's infancy; it simply starts when the hero is already an adult (like most stories do).

A World in four acts

English writer E. M. Forster (1879-1970) said, "'The king died and then the queen died' is a story. 'The king died, and then the queen died of grief' is a plot."

I respectfully disagree.

"The king died and then the queen died" is a chronology. "The king died, and then the queen died of grief" is almost a plot, but not quite.

So what's missing?

Well, in their most elemental form, stories (or plots) have three parts:
1) Something happens (Act I – Setup).
2) Someone does something about it (Act II – Confrontation).
3) Either things change for good, or not (Act III – Resolution).

Anything less than this, and what you have is just a chronicle. For that reason, in this book I divide the Hero's Journey in the following acts and sub-acts:

Act	Stages	What happens here:
0 - Hook	1	You grab your audience's attention.
1 - Setup	2 to 62	You introduce the problem and the characters around it.
2.1 - Reaction	63 to 118	The Hero rolls with the punches.
2.2 - Epiphany	119	The Hero finally understands what's really going on and what to do.
2.3 - Proaction	120 to 142	The Hero implements a plan. It fails.
3 - Climax	143 to 184	The forces of Good and Evil collide.
4 - Dénouement	186 to 195	You write an unforgettable ending.

Stages versus scenes

How much space, in paragraphs or pages, should each stage take in your novel?

If you write one page for each stage in this book, you have a 195-page novel right there. But it doesn't work like that.

Some stages might take several pages, and others might only need a single sentence. It all depends on the relative importance of each stage in a particular story.

Consider the following, though:

- **The general sequence.** In some stories the timeline jumps around a lot between past, present and future; the story itself, though, must have a consistent causal chain. The Call to Adventure can only happen *after* the Hero has met the Mentor; the Final Battle must take place at the end, and so on, even if the temporal sequence in which these events are presented to the reader is not linear.

- **Some scenes represent more than one stage.** On average, movies and novels have sixty scenes; consequently (also on average) each scene comprises about three stages of the Hero's Journey. For example, when Han Solo joins the battle at the end of *Star Wars: Episode IV - A New Hope,* three different stages are represented by that one action (see stages 165, 166, and 167 of this book).

- **Some stages don't translate directly into scenes.** These stages represent arcs, checkpoints, etc. (see Types of Stages, below). This is where authors must use their talent to transcend clichés.

Clichés are the enemy

The 195 stages form the master structure of great stories. But two pitfalls lie ahead:

- **Predictability.** When I watch a movie, I always know when the Mentor is going to die, whether or not the Hero is going to pass a particular test, and so on. In fact, I am gladly surprised when something happens that I didn't see coming.
- **Unconscious plagiarism.** If you write a novel following the stages to the letter, you may end up with a rip-off of *Harry Potter* or *Star Wars* on your hands—and a lawsuit at your doorstep. That would be a pity, because even if all stories are fundamentally similar, there is a myriad of great ways to tell them, waiting to be discovered by the next imaginative author.

Take advantage of the 195 stages, but stay creative because novels written by numbers only mimic the real thing. Don't just follow the stages; make them sing and dance for you.

Types of stages

Plot points

These stages mark the imminent beginning of a new act:

    061 – First Epiphany
    119 – Second Epiphany
    142 – Third Epiphany

These epiphanies emerge from revelations: It's the acquisition of new knowledge or information that generates the change. These stages are printed on gray pages.

Repetitive stages

A great story takes the Hero—and the audience—to new, exciting landscapes. Every time a border is crossed (like a police checkpoint, a jump between dimensions, or just a door), the Hero does the following:

- **Encounters a guardian.** It can be a security check, a centurion, a monster, a padlock, a password, or just a lazy dog sleeping in the way, belly up. These guardians are tests.

- **Discovers new things.** New smells, different colors, changing seasons, strange animals, or just underwear on the floor; in short, the Hero encounters things relevant to that new place.
- **Evolves.** And the Hero's external appearance reflects this inner growth. The Hero might change into new clothes or a disguise, armor, a space suit, a swimsuit, etc.

Consider reintroducing these stages whenever the setting changes:

006 – Foreshadowing
026 – The Hero's Weakness
027 – The Lie the Hero Believes
044 – Transmogrifications
065 – New Clothes
066 – Transitions
072 – No Going Back
068 – Guardians
139 – Ticking Clock

Now and then, we all fantasize about disappearing for a while, and transitions are a great chance to allow your readers to go on an imaginary trip. Use that opportunity well, and they will love you for it.

Particularly important is 006 – Foreshadowing. To paraphrase Chekhov, if there is a rifle hanging on the wall in the first act, it absolutely must go off in the second act. If the rifle is not going to be fired, it shouldn't be hanging there. Planting and removing elements ones is mostly done during re-writings, because you will only know what's important and what's not after you've finished the first draft.

Symbolic stages

These stages appeal to archetypal symbolism. Though almost subliminal, they *are* there, even if you don't notice them at first.

084 – Snake Symbolism
090 – Blindness Symbolism

Joker stages

Joker stages introduce either relief or a touch of humor. Place them wherever they best serve the story. I use them to dissipate any excessive tension created by the most intense passages:

   098 – The Awkward Innocent
   144 – The Reluctant Aid
   145 – The Comedic Relief
   159 – The Oblivious Innocent
   187 – Ally Is Fine

How to use *The Ultimate Hero's Journey*

Use it to plot. You can use the stages either to develop the big picture of your story or to define scenes to the finest detail—or both (which is what I do).

Use it to defeat writer's block. Getting lost in Act Two is pretty common because it is usually the longest act. But with this book you will never get stuck there again; just jump to the next stage and continue writing or plotting from there. Later on, everything will fall into place as you fill any remaining holes.

Use it to become a better critic. You don't have to write a novel or a script, of course; you can simply read this book for learning and enjoyment. But something interesting will happen: You will become a sharper observer. Granted, you will be harder to please, because weak passages and plot holes will be more evident to you. But you will also gain appreciation for subtle, masterful touches. I promise that after reading this book, you'll enjoy much more everything you read or watch.

Spoiler alert

I took examples from movies because watching a 90-minute film is easier than analyzing a 400-page novel. Each movie follows its own timeline, of course, so the 195 stages won't necessarily list the scenes of those movies in perfect sequence.

The first three movies are *Star Wars*, *The Matrix*, and *Harry Potter*, which are similar to each other in that they all narrate the prophecy of the Chosen One. I use examples taken from the first installment in each series, although on occasion I will refer to later parts of their sagas.

Then I include a drama and a comedy, too. The drama is *Sideways*, a multi-award winner novel and movie that shows how the Hero's Journey works in a human story. There are no chosen ones here, no villains wearing black capes, no venerable mentors—just life-like characters incarnating those roles in a complex way, albeit in a simple story. The comedy is *Dodgeball*, which shows how the stages can be satirized to humorous effect.

Last but not least

- I use the terms "dark side" and "light side" (lowercase) to represent the Freudian *id* and *superego* (i.e., the bad guys and the good guys). When referring to *Star Wars*' Dark Side, I use uppercase.
- For simplicity, some sentences use the masculine gender, but it also includes women. Sometimes I say "he," and sometimes I say "she"; I mean both. In fact, the heroines of my own stories are women (and so is the "knight" depicted in the back cover of this book).
- Repetitions are intentional; good stories always have motifs that echo through the pages. And please excuse the occasional expletive; they are never mine, but come from quoting passages. (Oh, you'll be fine.)

So, let's start.

(Page intentionally left blank.)

Jiu-Jitsu? I'm going to learn Jiu-Jitsu?"
—Neo (The Matrix, 1999)

THE ULTIMATE
HERO'S JOURNEY

(See page 198 for a complete list of stages.)

Hints for an easy navigation:

STAGE (AFTER CAMPBELL)

ACT NUMBER

ROAD OF TRIALS — The Ultimate Hero's Journey — ACT **2.1**

091 – Attack 4: Interrogation

The Villain tries to extract information from the Hero.

Description:

The Hero has entered the radar of the Villain. However, the Villain hasn't yet realized the magnitude of the threat the Hero poses.

In this stage, we see the dark side's methods up close. There is an interrogation or a demand, but the Hero refuses to collaborate, even under duress.

Examples:

Star Wars: Darth Vader enters Leia's cell and demands to know the location of the Rebel base. A scary interrogation drone with a needle hovers toward the Princess. She resists the torture.

The Matrix: Neo is interrogated by the Agents. He gives them the finger. Later on, Morpheus will resist their terrible methods, too.

Harry Potter: Just before the Sorting Hat ceremony, Malfoy tries to recruit Harry for his cabal. Harry refuses.

Sideways: Jack tries to put Miles into party mood. Miles just want to go back to the motel and crash.

Dodgeball: White tries to seduce Kate. She says, "Sorry, I vomited a little bit inside my mouth."

Related:
033 – Attack 3: The Hero Resists
092 – Attack 5: Spying

THE STAGE NUMBER IS ALWAYS THE SAME AS THE PAGE NUMBER

001 – The Hook

The bad guy is either on top or getting there.

Description:

The Hook grabs the attention of your audience. The first pages have to be gripping, and the first line should be memorable.

What happens here? The antagonist is in power and in pursuit; he suppresses every resistance and eliminates every threat.

Recurring motif: strong contrasts; for example, light and darkness, or black and white clothes. Like a visual yin and yang, the contrasts represent the opposing sides of the theme (i.e., good versus evil). Avoid too many explanations; keep it dynamic and mysterious.

Examples:

Star Wars: Bright lasers explode against the blackness of space: An immense destroyer is in pursuit. A masked figure dressed in black—boards a smaller vessel. Who is that, and what is he looking for?

The Matrix: Total blackness. Suddenly, a flashlight blinds us. We see many policemen converging on an abandoned hotel. What is going on? (Also, note that pretty much everyone dresses in black or white).

Harry Potter: It's already dark in Surrey. An old man in dark robes uses a magical gizmo to suck up the light from the street lamps. A stray cat transforms into an elderly witch dressed in black. Can they trust Hagrid (whoever that is) with something as important as this?

Sideways: Total blackness. A knock on the door. A man in white underwear opens the door, and the sunlight blinds him. Who is he?

Dodgeball: Welcome to Globo Gym, a place full of model-like customers wearing black sport outfits. Their motto: *"We're Better Than You—and We Know it!"*

Related:

153 – Back to the Hook

002 – The Villain
We get to see the power of the dark side.

Description:

Enter the Villain. The display of power makes us realize that the dark side is either on top or mounting forces.

This guy is not the Über-Villain, though (like Sauron, Palpatine, Moriarty, and other master villains that pull the strings from the shadows).

Recurring motif: The number three, which has extensive mythical connotations. See how many times you spot it in the examples below.

Examples:

Star Wars: Darth Vader, number three in command after Governor Tarkin and the Emperor himself, gives his men the order to kill everyone on board, except for the princess, who is taken prisoner.

The Matrix: Three men in black suits arrive at the scene. They are supernaturally powerful, but they're not the ultimate Villain. Their intention is to kill a woman who's hiding inside the hotel. Her name is Trinity (note the number three in her name). She is in room #303.

Harry Potter: The three wizards leave a baby at the doorstep of the only family he has: Three of "the worst sort of muggles imaginable." Still, they are nothing compared with the villains we will meet.

Sideways: As we will discover, the enemy in this story is Miles's own personality.

Dodgeball: Enter hilarious and ridiculous White Goodman: Owner, operator, and founder (three functions) of Globo Gym America Corp. Wait, is that hairdo for real?

Related:

074 – The Traitor
081 – The False Enemy
125 – The Über-Villain

INCITING EVENT · The Ultimate Hero's Journey · ACT **1**

003 – The (Sleeping) Hero

We meet the Hero, who is largely oblivious to what's going on.
And he's sleeping.

Description:

Recurring motif: Sleeping and dreaming are symbols of the Hero's pending awakening. The Hero still carries his Ordinary World name.

Superhero movies usually show the Hero in his childhood or adolescence, a narrative that involves bullies, high-school sweethearts, and an explanation of how the superpower was acquired. It's also commonplace for superheroes to be millionaires: Bruce Wayne, Tony Stark, Danny Rand, Oliver Queen, Francis Xavier, etc. (The ones in the examples below aren't millionaires, though).

Examples:

Star Wars: Meet Luke Skywalker, a young man living in his uncle's farm. He's not shown sleeping because, unlike the rest of the ones below, he is a *willing* Hero—eager to go into adventure.

The Matrix: Meet Thomas A. Anderson, employee by day and hacker by night. He fell asleep at his computer after hours spent online looking for a man called Morpheus.

Harry Potter: Meet Harry. He is a sweet kid living with his uncle, aunt, and bully of a cousin. He is asleep until his aunt angrily bangs at the door of the cupboard under the stairs—that's his "room".

Sideways: Meet Miles Raymond. He overslept, and he's already late.

Dodgeball: Meet Peter La Fleur. He is sleeping on the couch, dreaming that the tickles in his testicles come from a woman. They come from Peter's dog, Crash, who's asking for food.

Related:
030 – The Goddess
038 – The Herald
046 – The Mentor

004 – The Hero's Anonymity
Nobody recognizes the Hero.

Description:

The Hero lives off the dark side's radar. His surrogate home is located in suburbia or some other remote place.

The Mentor is the only one who knows about the One (or will soon, thanks to some special mark—see stage 010).

Recurring motif: The number one, a symbol of the Hero being the One—a role he will step into as soon as he stops living in hiding.

Examples:

Star Wars: Luke lives in Tatooine, a planet on the outer rim of the galaxy. During his first scene the word "one" is said no less than eight times.

The Matrix: Neo—whose name is an anagram of "one"—lives in a suburban one-room apartment (which says "101" on the door).

Harry Potter: Harry lives in a suburban house, in a generic neighborhood. Today is his cousin's eleventh birthday. Harry himself is almost eleven, too.

Sideways: Miles lives in a suburban house in Los Angeles. It is almost 11 o'clock.

Dodgeball: Peter lives in a suburban house in Los Angeles, too. The rule about the number one is changed for the number five, instead: It's 5 minutes to noon, there are 5 messages in the answering machine, his water supply will be cut at 5:00 p.m., and the DVDs he rented (among them, *Backdoor Patrol 5*) are overdue. But note this: The Hero plus five friends are what's needed to form *one* winning dodgeball team.

Related:
010 – The Sign of the One

005 – The Hero's Talent
We get to see a token of the Hero's superpower.

Description:

The Hero's talent is not necessarily a superpower, of course. But the Hero must have some ability that no one else has. Such talent, however, is still untrained, intuitive, and impulsive.

In this stage we see the other side of the coin, too: The Hero's Weakness (stage 026). so the audience can empathize with the Hero, because of both his remarkable talent and his human flaw.

The Hero's story is bound to that of the Villain: They are basically the same guy, only on opposite sides of the theme (009 – Mutual Creation).

Examples:

Star Wars: Luke Skywalker is a hard-working, kind, and courageous young man. He is an outstanding pilot, too. However, he's also a little too self-confident, which gets him in trouble. Anakin Skywalker (Darth Vader) was like that, too.

The Matrix: Neo's talent is bound to his very existence: He *is* The One. But he is skeptical, too, and clueless about what's going on in the world—if such a thing exists.

Harry Potter: Harry can talk to snakes and make things disappear. Harry's weakness is his cluelessness about his family, about magic, and about himself. Tom Riddle (Voldemort) was exactly like that, too.

Sideways: Miles is a writer and a teacher; he is very good with words. He solves the *New York Times* crossword puzzle while driving, which is very irresponsible.

Dodgeball: Everybody likes Peter La Fleur; he is good with people. But he is also indolent.

Related:
011 – The Hero's Immaturity; 026 – The Hero's Weakness

006 – Foreshadowing

You have to put the gun in the mantelpiece before it can go off in chapter sixteen.

Description:

Look for essential details of your story and then plant some elements of anticipation like artifacts, people, or situations.

Strive to include every element at least twice, and with purpose. De-clutter your prose by removing unimportant bits. Make your foreshadowing subtle, almost subliminal.

Examples:

Star Wars: Anakin gets his arm cut off by Count Dooku; from then on, he uses a robotic arm that foreshadows his transformation into Vader. Then Luke also gets his arm cut off in a lightsaber duel, and a robotic hand replaces it. Will he also become a Sith Lord, or will he stay true to the light side? That's the essential dilemma Luke faces.

The Matrix: Neo arrives late at work. His boss tells him, "You believe that you are special, that somehow the rules do not apply to you. The time has come to make a choice, Mr. Anderson." And the story is about The One, for whom the rules don't apply and who fights the Machines' domination precisely through choice.

Let me include here an example from a different movie: ***Raiders of the Lost Ark.*** In the first act, Indiana Jones escapes the indigenous warriors in the jungle, but when he gets in his plane there's a big snake inside the cockpit. He *hates* snakes. In the second act, he is thrown into an Egyptian chamber. And what's down there? Not one, but hundreds of the most venomous snakes in the world, of course. (By the way, that's one of the many snake symbolisms in that movie).

Related:

084 – Snake Symbolism.

007 – The Surrogate Parents
The Hero lives in an ordinary home.

Description:

The surrogate family may be good people, but they represent the Ordinary World, which contrasts with the Hero's prodigious capacities. They deny the Hero's true origin and press the Hero not to follow destiny.

Examples:

Star Wars: The harvest is all Uncle Owen cares about. He needs Luke's help for just another year. Last year he said the same thing, of course.

The Matrix: Neo doesn't have a surrogate family, just a boss who orders him to arrive at work on time.

Harry Potter: The Dursleys are the epitome of suburban mediocrity. They deny the magic world, repress that nature in Harry, and they call Harry's parents "freaks"—or worse.

Sideways: Jack is an actor, but Mike Erganian, his future father-in-law, wants him to work in the real-estate business.

Dodgeball: The role of the Surrogate Parent in this case is performed by Gordon's mail-order wife—she is the surrogate parent to Gordon children. She hates and humiliates Gordon.

Related:

008 – It's a Hard-Knock Life
021 – Stuck in the Ordinary World
032 – Resistance to the Separation

008 – It's a Hard-Knock Life
The Hero follows a mundane but strenuous routine.

Description:

Willing heroes (like Luke Skywalker) live well under their capacities; unwilling heroes (like Neo or Harry) are pretty much treated like slaves.

Soon, the Hero will be called to something bigger than this. Despite the terrible ordeals in store, the Adventure World will ultimately be a path to freedom.

Examples:

Star Wars: Luke receives orders from both his uncle and aunt ("Clean the droids," "Look for one that speaks Bocce," etc.)

The Matrix: "You are a slave, Neo," Morpheus will tell him. Neo lives in a prison he cannot see, smell, or touch: A simulation of what he believes is the real world.

Harry Potter: "Just cook the breakfast, and try not to burn anything," Aunt Petunia tells Harry. He is treated almost like a slave.

Sideways: Miles is told to move the car from the entrance of his condo so the painters can work.

Dodgeball: Jason is bullied, Gordon is abused by his wife, Steve is crazy, and Owen can't find a girlfriend. They will all find redemption in the Adventure World.

Related:

007 – The Surrogate Parents
020 – The Hero's Day Job
021 – Stuck in the Ordinary World
032 – Resistance to the Separation

009 – Mutual Creation
Hero and Villain are two sides of the same coin,
both opposing and complementary.

Description:

The Hero and the Villain share a common origin. They became what they are because of their actions and, even more importantly, their interactions. In particular, they cannot eliminate the other without destroying themselves (literally or otherwise).

This stage is tricky to place in a story; in long movies sagas it is usually left for the second part.

Examples:

Star Wars: Anakin and Padmé had Luke; but as far as Anakin (Vader) knows, his son and Padmé died in childbirth—which is why Anakin turned to the Dark Side.

The Matrix: Humans created the Machines, and the Machines created Neo, a human, to solve the inherent imbalance in The Matrix. Both sides are mutually dependent.

Harry Potter: Harry's resilience against Voldemort was created by the Dark Lord's killing curse that bounced on Lily Potter. If Voldemort kills Harry, he kills himself, and vice versa.

Bonus Example:

Batman (1989): This movie offers a classic example. The Joker's persona emerges when Jack Napier falls in a tank full of chemicals during a fight against Batman. Conversely, Batman's persona emerges from Bruce Wayne's trauma: His parents where killed years before, in a dark alley, by… Jack Napier.

Related:
025 – The Hero's Ghost
048 – Historic Battle

010 – The Sign of the One
The Hero is recognized by a symbol he carries.

Description:

The Sign of the One is the way the Mentor recognizes the Hero.

It can be a tattoo, like in *The Fifth Element*, *The Girl with the Dragon Tattoo*, or *Popeye* (1980). It can be a real scar, like in Harry Potter, or a metaphorical one, like in Dexter. Sometimes it can be an extraordinary ability, like Frodo's resilience to the power of the Ring.

In this stage the sign is only seen by the Hero (in a mirror, for example), or it's noticed by someone else but in a private situation. The sign usually remains concealed for other people.

Examples:

Star Wars: Luke's mark is his name: Skywalker. Obi-Wan knows it too well, because he was there when Luke was born.

The Matrix: Neo's mark is invisible: His digital code. Morpheus just *knows* Neo is The One.

Harry Potter: Harry is famous for his scar, which is usually covered by the hair falling on his forehead. He shows the scar to Ron when they are alone in the train compartment.

Sideways: No signs of the One, here. These are totally normal people.

Dodgeball: The Average Joe's team is formed by the most average guys ever. No signs of the One here, either.

Related:
049 – The Prophecy Is Shared
050 – The Prophecy Is Incomplete

011 – The Hero's Immaturity
The Hero has a lot of room for improvement.

Description:

The Hero hasn't yet integrated the special power. It is either repressed, ignored, or resented.

We get to see a display of that power, but it's associated to some shortcoming, which is in turn a consequence of the Hero's Weakness.

Examples:

Star Wars: Luke bravely scouts and fights the Sand People; he gets his butt handed to him, though.

The Matrix: Neo is recognized by the Oracle as cuter than she thought but "not as bright, though."

Harry Potter: Harry speaks with snakes, but he doesn't even realize he is speaking in Parseltongue. He doesn't even recognize his own magic powers.

Sideways: Miles is good with words, but he uses them to lie, make excuses, and avoid conflict (see stage 015 – Cheating to Get By).

Dodgeball: Peter is so lazy that he hasn't collected any gym membership fees in thirteen months. He is the natural leader of his group, but he's also totally disinterested in the role—or any role, for that matter.

Related:
005 – The Hero's Talent
012 – The Hero's Ignorance
026 – The Hero's Weakness

012 – The Hero's Ignorance
Destiny awaits, but the Hero has no idea where to start.

Description:

The Hero is trapped in a grim routine (solitude, job dissatisfaction, hardships) in a world that's totally unsympathetic to that situation. No authorities, elders, or anyone else can solve the problem, because the problem is systemic.

This is not a "fish out of water" feeling, because the Hero has already adapted to the Ordinary World; what the Hero feels is a lack of purpose.

Examples:

Star Wars: Luke's days are wasted as a farmer. He wants to contact the Rebellion, but he doesn't know how. His Uncle pressures him to keep up with his routine.

The Matrix: Neo's days are wasted away as a corporate employee. He knows that something is wrong with the world, but he doesn't know what it is. His boss pressures him to keep up with his routine.

Harry Potter: Harry's life is wasting away in Little Whinging. Poor Harry—he knows nothing about anything.

Dodgeball: Peter's life is an ode to laziness. Why have any dreams if you can fail to achieve them?

Related:
005 – The Hero's Talent
011 – The Hero's Immaturity
026 – The Hero's Weakness

013 – The Mentor Awaits
When the student is ready, the teacher will show up—but not just yet.

Description:

The Mentor watches both the problem with the world (the Villain) and its solution (the Hero), but always from a distance.

Sometimes the one watching is the Herald—a character that will guide the Hero to the meeting with the Mentor.

The meeting between the Mentor and the Hero will only happen when the Hero is mature enough for the call and when the Villain is looking elsewhere.

Examples:

Star Wars: It's no coincidence that Ben Kenobi lives around the corner from Luke. The old Jedi master hid the boy from Vader and stayed not far away from the farm, waiting for the right moment.

The Matrix: Neo spends his nights looking for Morpheus, but Morpheus spent his entire life looking for The One. Trinity, a Goddess acting as Herald for now, watches him, waiting for the right moment to make contact.

Harry Potter: Dumbledore will send Harry the invitation to attend Hogwarts as soon as Harry is eleven. Until then, the boy must remain anonymous (stage 004 – The Hero's Anonymity).

Sideways: "I was beginning to think it was never going to happen," Miles says about the wine trip he and Jack are about to start.

Dodgeball: Patches O'Houlihan observes events from a corner of a restaurant. He has to wait until White Goodman has left.

Related:
046 – The Mentor
047 – Quick Introductions

014 – The World in Decline
"Alternative Facts"

Description:

Winter arrives, poverty ensues, and disease spreads. The powers in place impose a fake, superficial order, but the world is not a nice place anymore.

The masses buy the Villain's lies. Or they don't, but only a few dare to oppose him.

Examples:

Star Wars: The Empire extends its grip to more and more systems across the galaxy with its terror tactics—all in the name of keeping the peace and fighting the separatists.

The Matrix: The world itself is a lie, a computer simulation designed to keep humanity under control.

Harry Potter: A nightmare is taking shape in the magic world, but the Ministry of Magic insists on denying Voldemort's return.

Sideways: "It's like a total nightmare," Miles says. "There's been all this work going on at my building, and I had a bunch of stuff to deal with this morning." It seems that at least the world around him is in decline.

Dodgeball: The Globo Gym TV advertisement is a parade of superficiality and vanity.

Related:
019 – Selfishness Is on the Rise
035 – The Villain's Dominion
087 – World under Surveillance

015 – Cheating to Get By

The immature Hero deals with the Ordinary World the easy way.

Description:

Tricks and cheats help the Hero deal with some day-to-day problems. But such strategy will only take you so far.

Examples:

Star Wars: Luke lies to his aunt and leaves saying he had things to do; actually, he went after R2D2, who escaped in search for Obi-Wan.

The Matrix: Neo makes money on the side by trafficking illegal digital experiences. "You are my savior, man, my own personal Jesus Christ," says one of his customers.

Harry Potter: Harry's magical powers manifest when he is angry or scared. Magic is not allowed in the muggle world, but he doesn't know that.

Sideways: Miles tells Jack that he's already on his way, but he hasn't even flossed, yet.

Dodgeball: Peter always takes the easiest path—if at all.

Bonus Example:

Star Trek (2009): This movie offers a classic example of this stage: The infamous Kobayashi Maru test. Cadet James T. Kirk passes by altering the test's no-win-scenario settings. Doing so, he fails to comprehend the lesson that self-sacrifice is expected from Federation captains. That scene foreshadows stage 181 – Atonement; his father died as a captain and a Hero, and Jim Kirk will face the same situation.

Related:

014 – The World in Decline
019 – Selfishness Is on the Rise
022 – The Hero's Goal

016 – The Mentor's Knowledge

*The Mentor sees a problem with the world,
a problem that everyone else ignores.*

Description:

The Mentor's knowledge compensates for the Hero's Ignorance. But the Mentor hasn't even been formally introduced, yet. So this stage is usually shown metaphorically, for example by separating the Mentor from the decadence of the Ordinary World.

Examples:

Star Wars: Obi-Wan lives as a hermit—i.e., separated from everything else. He knows about Luke and Leia and how they can defeat the Empire.

The Matrix: Morpheus knows the truth about the world. He lives in the real world, not connected to the Matrix.

Harry Potter: Dumbledore knows that Voldemort is back and that Harry is the only hope against the rise of evil. The old wizard spends most of his time alone in his office.

Sideways: Miles knows about Jack's second thoughts regarding the wedding; conversely, Jack knows Miles's dark side and how to manage it. They both act as mentors of each other.

Dodgeball: Patches O'Houlihan explains how to win a dodgeball match: "You've gotta grab it by its haunches and hump it into submission. That's the only way."

Related:
034 – The Mentor's Faith

017 – Denial of the Premise

The reason behind the world's problem is denied or ridiculed.

Description:

Ordinary People are in denial. Some can't see the truth; some choose not to.

In this stage, some Ordinary World characters scoff at the truth. If the story is about ghosts, for example, someone will say, "Ghosts don't exist," or "UFO's are not real," or "There's no such thing as demonic possession".

Immediately after that, something happens that proves them wrong.

Examples:

Star Wars: Admiral verbally attacks Vader. "Your sad devotion to that ancient religion has not helped you conjure up the stolen data tapes," he says. Then Vader Force-chokes him for that comment.

The Matrix: Neo himself refuses to believe the truth. "I don't believe it. I don't believe it," he says after Morpheus reveals to him the truth about the world.

Harry Potter: Uncle Vernon screams, "There's no such thing as magic!" Seconds later, and to Harry's amusement, Hagrid uses his magic umbrella to put an actual pig's tail on Dudley's butt. The three Dursleys run around screaming.

Sideways: Miles tells his ex-wife, Victoria, "I just heard about you getting married, and I was taken aback. Hard to believe."

Dodgeball: Peter doesn't believe that playing a game will save the gym. He says, "You know what's sad? Six grown men playing dodgeball."

Related:
014 – The World in Decline
016 – The Mentor's Knowledge

018 – Attack 1: Insult

Either the Hero or the Mentor are insulted or called names.

Description:

The decadence of the world also shows in the way people treat each other: Kindness is replaced by callousness, or even insults.

The Hero experiences such change first hand, but the provocation goes unanswered either because the insulted character is absent, or because he doesn't care, or because he can't risk an escalation of the problem.

Examples:

Star Wars: Ben Kenobi is called *in absentia* a "strange hermit," "crazy," and "old" half a dozen times.

The Matrix: The police lieutenant tells the Agents, "You give me that 'juris-my-dick-tion' crap, you can cram it up your ass." Luckily for the policeman, the Agents don't answer to that.

Harry Potter: Harry is verbally abused by his surrogate family. They also call Dumbledore a "crackpot old fool." Harry can't answer to them.

Sideways: Jack opens a bottle of a rare champagne inside the car, spilling the best part of it. Miles says, "you fucking derelict!" Jack doesn't care—he just want to celebrate his last week of freedom before the wedding.

Dodgeball: White Goodman tells Peter, "In thirty days I'll be bulldozing that shit-heap you call a gym into permanent nothingness." Peter ignores the provocation.

Related:
028 – Attack 2: Physical Damage

019 – Selfishness is on the Rise
The world has become an egoistic place.

Description:

This is yet another symptom of the general decadence. We see a theft, a denial to share, unfair competition, or some other selfish attitude.

How dramatic this stage is depends on the genre. It can simply be represented by someone trying to take a potato chip from a friend's plate and getting playfully reprimanded for it.

Sometimes the selfishness is showed by contrast, presenting an act of kindness or generosity that's perceived as a rare event.

Examples:

Star Wars: The Sand People (criminals, thieves, and assassins) lurk around, as do the Jawas, who steal and sell droids.

The Matrix: A messenger delivers a parcel to Neo. Before leaving, the guy cheerfully says, "Have a nice day!" Neo looks at him and tries to decide if the guy was mocking him.

Harry Potter: Harry's spoiled brat of a cousin makes a scene: He only got thirty-six birthday presents. "Last year I got thirty-seven!"

Sideways: In the movie script, Christine calls Jack on the cell phone just five minutes after he left; she insists in discussing some unimportant seating arrangement for the wedding. They have an argument.

Dodgeball: During the cheerleading auditions, Jason is paired with a hyper-obese girl by his rival, Derek. When she falls butt-first on Jason's face, Derek laughs at him.

Related:
014 – The World in Decline
015 – Cheating to Get By
022 – The Hero's Goal

020 – The Hero's Day Job
A lion among the sheep.

Description:

Destiny has something reserved for the Hero, but right now, the Hero is engaged in a mundane job—most commonly, continuing in the Surrogate Parent's profession.

The Hero is pretty good at it, but is also underutilized and underappreciated.

Examples:

Star Wars: The Rebellion will find Luke soon. For the time being he has to deal with humidifiers, droids, and harvests.

The Matrix: The Resistance will find Neo soon, but right now he works in a generic cubicle in a non-descript office building.

Harry Potter: Harry Potter is just another suburban kid. Hagrid will come for him soon.

Sideways: Miles works as a high-school literature teacher. His dream of becoming a published author must wait for another time.

Dodgeball: Peter La Fleur is the owner of the crappiest gym in town, but he will end up owning much more than that.

Related:

021 – Stuck in the Ordinary World
032 – Resistance to the Separation

INCITING EVENT — The Ultimate Hero's Journey — ACT 1

021 – Stuck in the Ordinary World
There is no change in sight, or so the Hero thinks.

Description:

The Hero longs to leave, but such longing is unconscious. In fact, later on, the Hero will refuse the offer to go into the adventure.

The Mentor and the Heralds are still out of the Hero's sight. The feeling that the Hero may never be up to the circumstance must sink in the audience's mind for now.

Examples:

Star Wars: Luke is denied the chance to go to the Academy. He stands up and motions to leave the room. His aunt asks, "Where are you going?" Luke complains, "It looks like I'm going nowhere."

The Matrix: Neo sits still in his cubicle, in front of his spent computer. He just sits in there, doing nothing.

Harry Potter: Harry is just a kid. Where would he go?

Sideways: Miles is divorced and childless. His novel keeps getting rejected, and his job sucks. He is stuck in a totally human situation.

Dodgeball: Peter La Fleur spends his days thinking, "If you don't have goals, you are never disappointed. And I tell you: It feels phenomenal." Yep, he's going nowhere.

Related:
008 – It's a Hard-Knock Life
032 – Resistance to the Separation

022 – The Hero's Goal

The Hero only wants to solve some immediate problem.

Description:

The Hero's current goal is nothing transcendental, but it's enough to put the Hero on the path to adventure. The Inciting Event (stage 029) will render both the goal and the associated problem irrelevant.

Examples:

Star Wars: Luke's goal is to attend the Academy, become a pilot, and join the Rebellion. Uncle Owen won't let him.

The Matrix: Neo's goal is to answer the question that drives him mad.

Harry Potter: Harry just wants to read the letter from Hogwarts. In this story, however, the strongest goals are Dumbledore's versus Voldemort's.

Sideways: Miles's goal is to go on vacation and forget his love wounds.

Dodgeball: Peter La Fleur has no goals at all. He expects nothing from life. Well, sex, maybe.

Related:

023 – The Hero's Desire
029 – The Inciting Event

INCITING EVENT — The Ultimate Hero's Journey — ACT **1**

023 – The Hero's Desire
The root of the Hero's problem.

Description:

This early in the story, the Hero's desire is either primal (revenge, money, escape, etc.), or mundane (avoiding ridicule, achieving fame, keeping a job, etc.)

Such desire will eventually evolve into something transcendental, but not just yet. Any higher, noble pursuit is only expressed in broad terms: To defend the country, to find love, etc.

Examples:

Star Wars: Luke wants to be free. Soon he will be fighting for freedom at a scale he doesn't imagine.

The Matrix: Neo wants to know what the Matrix is. Little does he know that the Matrix is the battlefield in which he will fight for humanity.

Harry Potter: Harry lacks friends, family, and knowledge—precisely the things he will find in his new school.

Sideways: Miles's failures put his desire in retreat: He increasingly finds pleasure only in wine.

Dodgeball: Peter has no desires. But he will end up betting it all for friendship.

Related:
022 – The Hero's Goal

024 – A Warning and a Threat

The Ordinary World reveals its controlling nature.

Description:

An Ordinary World's authority demands compliance with a rule. Should the warning be ignored, some form of punishment will ensue.

The Hero acquiesces silently; the moment to go into full rebellion mode hasn't arrived yet.

Examples:

Star Wars: Uncle Owen orders Luke to clean up the droids before dinner: "You can waste time with your friends when your chores are done." Luke doesn't answer.

The Matrix: "Either you choose to be at your desk on time from this day forth," Neo's boss warns him, "or you choose to find yourself another job." Neo says he understands.

Harry Potter: "I'm warning you now, boy," threatens Uncle Vernon before the visit to the zoo. "Any funny business, any at all, and you won't have any meals for a week." Harry doesn't answer.

Sideways: Jack asks why pinot noir is white. Miles warns him: "Jesus. Don't ask questions like that up in the wine country. They'll think you're a moron." Jack doesn't answer.

Dodgeball: White Goodman threatens, "You've got 30 days to make $50,000, or your gym becomes my gym." Peter condescends, which only irritates White more.

Related:

018 – Attack 1: Insult
028 – Attack 2: Physical Damage

INCITING EVENT — The Ultimate Hero's Journey — **ACT 1**

025 – The Hero's Ghost

We learn about what happened to the Hero's real parents.

Description:

The story about the Hero's Ghost is usually told in three steps:

1) In this stage we learn about a traumatic event (a lost love, an accident, a crime, etc.) that happened to the Hero or to the Hero's parents. However, this account is either false or incomplete.

2) Later on, in stage 048 – Historic Battle, we hear a second version that is closer to the truth, but still incomplete.

3) Somewhere in Act 3, the full truth and how intimately connected it is to the Hero's existence and mission is revealed.

This stage represents the first step in the sequence.

Examples:

Star Wars: Luke was told that his father was a navigator on a freighter. Luke knows nothing about his mother.

The Matrix: (Not applicable).

Harry Potter: Harry believes his parents died in a car accident.

Sideways: Miles sees a picture of his deceased father. Actor Paul Giamatti's subtle expression of guilt and nostalgia cannot be put into words. Nothing else is said on the matter.

Dodgeball: (Not applicable).

Related:
009 – Mutual Creation
048 – Historic Battle

026 – The Hero's Weakness
Nobody's perfect.

Description:

The Weakness shows the childish side of the Hero: Immaturity, irresponsibility, and stubbornness. It symbolizes the inner dimension of the theme, the Hero's internal struggle.

In any case, the Weakness has to be something the audience can identify with; don't make your Hero a pervert or a coward, and don't make the Weakness morally disgusting.

The Weakness will be overcome in stage 171 – The Hero Lets Go.

Examples:

Star Wars: Luke's overconfidence interferes with his trust in the Force. That same cockiness will make him wander alone through the desert, getting attacked by the Sand People.

The Matrix: Neo's Weakness is disbelief. He doesn't believe Morpheus' explanation, nor the Oracle's prediction, nor that he is The One.

Harry Potter: Harry's Weakness is ignorance and a disregard for authority, which gets him in nine kinds of trouble.

Sideways: Miles is like a kid: He lies, steals from his mother, and uses avoidance strategies.

Dodgeball: Peter's Weakness is his total lack of motivation. If nothing is worth taking risks for, how can anything have any value at all?

Related:

027 – The Lie the Hero Believes
171 – The Hero Lets Go

027 – The Lie the Hero Believes
The Hero's paradigm is wrong.

Description:

The most basic assumptions of the Hero about who he is and what the world is like are simply wrong.

This mistaken paradigm is a consequence of the fundamental lie he believes in, which in turn is a consequence of his Weakness (stage 026).

The Lie is not refuted here; it will be taken care of by the Hero's character arc.

Examples:

Star Wars: Luke trusts his abilities as a pilot and little else. He ignores everything about the Force, including how intertwined the Dark Side is in his own personal history.

The Matrix: The Lie Neo believes in is: "I'm just another guy. I'm not The One."

Harry Potter: Harry is not wrong but ignorant: He doesn't know anything about the magic world.

Sideways: Miles sees the World through the somber glasses of his depression and negativity.

Dodgeball: Peter believes that taking risks doesn't pay. He doesn't realize that avoiding risks pays even less.

Related:
026 – The Hero's Weakness

028 – Attack 2: Physical Damage
The Hero suffers a physical attack.

Description:

We established that the Ordinary World is a mediocre and selfish place, but now it also becomes violent. This attack fuels the Hero's unconscious need to do something about it.

The Hero tries to fight back but is overpowered.

Examples:

Star Wars: Luke is attacked by the Sand People; he is hit and left unconscious.

The Matrix: Neo gets arrested, pinned down, and a tracking device is inserted in his body.

Harry Potter: Uncle Vernon pulls Harry's hair.

Sideways: Miles and Jack almost get hit by a golf ball shot at them by some bullies.

Dodgeball: Plenty of physical pain is shown throughout the movie. My favorite part is when the mean Girl Scouts wipe the floor with the guys during the regional qualifying match. I cringed a lot.

Related:

018 – Attack 1: Insult
033 – Attack 3: The Hero Resists

029 – The Inciting Event
Things start to move faster.

Description:

Something happens to the Hero; something intriguing, related to the core of the premise. This event sets everything in motion.

This stage doesn't answer any questions; it creates them.

Examples:

Star Wars: Luke discovers a holo-message hidden in a droid his uncle just bought. He thinks the message is for the Rebellion.

The Matrix: The police and the Agents arrive at Neo's office to arrest him. The cell-phone brought by the FedEx messenger rings. It is Morpheus, who offers to help Neo escape.

Harry Potter: Uncle Vernon destroys a letter directed to Harry. Then thousands of owls bring more copies. The letters fly around the house, and more of them come flying through the windows, the door's mail slot, and even the fireplace.

Sideways: Jack, who's getting married in a week, arranges a date with two attractive women for him and his (depressed and recently divorced) friend. How's that ever going to work well?

Dodgeball: The bank assigned Kate Veatch, a beautiful and intelligent lawyer, to work on Average Joe's foreclosure.

Related:
030 – The Goddess
059 – Pushing Event

030 – The Goddess
The Inciting Event has a woman at its center.

Description:

The feminine is associated with creative energy, with the origin of life. And in fiction, too, there is usually a woman at the center of the story, setting things in motion.

If the Goddess happens to be the romantic interest for the Hero, don't rush things between them, no matter the initial attraction.

Note that at this point the Hero and the Goddess haven't met, yet—except in romantic fiction.

Recurring motif: The concept of hope.

Examples:

Star Wars: Leia's holographic message starts it all. The message talks about hope.

The Matrix: Trinity watches Neo. Everyone hopes he is The One, but she doesn't have to hope: She knows it. The other Goddess in the story, the Oracle, knows it as well.

Harry Potter: Harry's power comes from the love of Lily, his mother. Thanks to her, Harry is The Boy Who Lived. But Harry will meet two additional goddesses: Professor McGonagall and Ginny Weasley. (Hermione acts a Goddess mainly in relation to Ron).

Sideways: Miles's traumas and depression stem from his divorce from Victoria, his affair with Brenda, and his falling in love with Maya—Goddesses everywhere.

Dodgeball: Kate will be the catalyst of Peter's awakening. Without her on the team, Average Joe's has no hope. She can't play, though, because of a conflict of interests (she works for White's bank).

Related:

076 – First Encounter with the Goddess

031 – A Storm Is Coming
The onset of evil can be felt in the air.

Description:

This stage introduces a sense of premonition, of something lingering in the atmosphere. This is just an intuition, not a triggering event; ordinary people don't experience this intuition—only some main character does.

Recurring motifs include big spaces and a character looking into the distance in suspicious anticipation.

Examples:

Star Wars: Luke scrutinizes the desert's horizon and says, "That little droid is going to cause me a lot of trouble." Indeed, it will.

The Matrix: Morpheus tells Neo, "You're here because you know something. You don't know what it is, but it's there—like a splinter in your mind, driving you mad."

Harry Potter: When McGonagall asks if the rumors about Harry's parents are true, Dumbledore confirms, "I'm afraid so, Professor. The good, and the bad."

Sideways: (Not applicable).

Dodgeball: Peter's car barely starts in the morning, and he says, "It's gonna be a good day." His intuition is wrong, of course.

Bonus Example:

The Lord of the Rings: The trilogy starts with this stage. Lady Galadriel says, "The world is changed. I feel it in the water. I feel it in the earth. I smell it in the air."

Related:
014 – The World in Decline

032 – Resistance to the Separation
The Hero arches away from the Surrogate Parents.
They disapprove.

Description:

The Hero will soon leave the Ordinary World behind, a fact foreshadowed by the distance the Hero takes from the surrogate family.

They resist the Hero's departure; not because of love but because of self-interest.

Examples:

Star Wars: Luke wants to go looking for Ben Kenobi. His uncle forbids it, saying, "Tomorrow, I want you to take that R2 unit to Anchorhead and have its memory erased. That'll be the end of it."

The Matrix: Neo has no family (surrogate or otherwise). The ones resisting his leaving the Matrix are the Machines, which are his "family," albeit in a strange way.

Harry Potter: Uncle Vernon knows that the letters are an invitation for Harry to attend Hogwarts, so he destroys them all.

Sideways: The resistance to the separation here is based on love, after all. Miles and Jack visited Miles's mother (it's her birthday), and she wants them to stay for breakfast the next morning with the rest of the family.

Dodgeball: The team wants to go to Las Vegas. In an inversion of roles, Peter is the one opposing the departure.

Related:
007 – The Surrogate Parents
021 – Stuck in the Ordinary World
039 – Unusual Places

033 – Attack 3: The Hero Resists

The Hero stands his ground for the first time.

Description:

The Hero loses patience and starts resisting the pushes. The Hero didn't react to the previous attacks, but the third time's the charm.

It doesn't work.

Examples:

Star Wars: Luke confronts Han Solo and his demands during their negotiation in the Cantina. It doesn't work: Han is promised even more money than he asked for.

The Matrix: Neo confronts the agents. He isn't intimidated by their "Gestapo crap." It doesn't work: They insert a tracking device through his abdomen.

Harry Potter: Harry disobeys Uncle Vernon and grabs one of the hundreds of letters flying around. It doesn't work: Harry gets locked in the cupboard under the stairs.

Sideways: Miles criticizes the wine at the place where Stephanie works to stop Jack from seducing her. It doesn't work: Jack arranges a date with her.

Dodgeball: Peter deflects White's verbal attacks. The expropriation process is in motion.

Related:

028 – Attack 2: Physical Damage
091 – Attack 4: Interrogation

034 – The Mentor's Faith

The Mentor trusts the Hero will face the challenges ahead.

Description:

The archetype of the Mentor represents wisdom. The Mentor also acts as a bridge between the Ordinary World and some Higher Realm; the Mentor defends the conviction about the Hero being the Chosen One despite objections from the other members of that select group.

Usually, the Goddess has access to that Higher Realm even though she doesn't belong in it.

Examples:

Star Wars: Obi-Wan, Yoda, and Senator Organa comprise the Higher Realm—the only ones who know the truth about Luke. In *Episode V – The Empire Strikes Back*, Obi-Wan defends his choices about Luke despite Yoda's disappointments in the young man.

The Matrix: The Oracle, The Architect, and Morpheus are the only ones who know the truth about Neo. Morpheus believes in Neo "so blindly that no one can convince him otherwise, not even me," the Oracle says.

Harry Potter: Dumbledore, McGonagall, and Snape are the only ones who know the truth about Harry. Dumbledore persists in his plan, despite the resistance from the other two professors.

Sideways: Miles and Jack both act as Mentors for each other. Despite their differences, they never lose faith in each other.

Dodgeball: Coach O'Houlihan forces Gordon to run across a highway: "If you can dodge traffic, you can dodge a ball." Although O'Houlihan believes in Gordon, he still gets hit by a car. Twice.

Related:

016 – The Mentor's Knowledge

INCITING EVENT — The Ultimate Hero's Journey — ACT 1

035 – The Villain's Dominion

Anyone who opposes the antagonist is persecuted or eliminated.

Description:

The Villain advances like a bulldozer.

Dictators imprison and kill opponents; asteroids destroy satellites and spaceships in their way; volcanoes lay waste on a small town; a jealous lover spreads lies. Villains, too, believe they are obeying a superior call, leaving no room for guilt or ethical considerations.

The Hero and the Goddess, however, have a special resilience to the destructive power of the dark side.

Examples:

Star Wars: Vader kills everyone on board the Corellian cruiser that transports Leia. He tortures her to find out the location of the missing droids and of the Rebel base, but she resists.

The Matrix: Agent Smith smashes a phone booth with a huge truck to kill Trinity, who escapes by a fraction of a second.

Harry Potter: Voldemort kills anyone who refuses to become a Death Eater, including Lily and James Potter. Trying to kill baby Harry didn't work as planned, though.

Sideways: Jack warns Miles, "I'm serious. Do not fuck with me. I am going to get laid before I settle down on Saturday." Miles resists, threatening to leave the trip.

Dodgeball: The Purple Cobras show off. The scary female Romanovian player knocks out a guy in the bar by throwing a ball at him. Later on, she fails to shoot Owen, though, because she fell in love with him.

Related:

036 – The Villain's Orders
136 – The Villain Rises

036 – The Villain's Orders
The intentions of the bad guy are clearer.

Description:

The Villain issues orders to the lieutenants. This happens in private, and the exchange makes the Villain's objectives more evident (his objectives, not his motives, yet).

This also shows the hierarchy of characters in the dark side.

Examples:

Star Wars: Darth Vader orders a search of the escape pod: The plans must be recovered at any cost. (We don't know yet what plans are they talking about).

The Matrix: Agent Smith orders a search for Neo. He is clearly the leader of the group of Agents. We don't know yet who Neo is, or why the Agents are looking for him.

Harry Potter: Professor Quirrell acts following Voldemort orders, of course. But that revelation is kept in reserve until the final battle.

Sideways: Just before going to dinner with the girls, Jack tells Miles, "If they want to drink merlot, we're drinking merlot." Miles refuses: "If anyone orders merlot, I'm leaving. I am not drinking any fucking merlot!" They both act like each other's Villain.

Dodgeball: White tells his lieutenant, Me'Shell: "Involuntary spasm! Enjoy the show! Now *you're* my bitch."

Related:

035 – The Villain's Dominion
136 – The Villain Rises

037 – Secret Message
"This message will self-destruct in five seconds."

Description:

The Hero receives a secret message. It can be a cryptic note, an anonymous e-mail, an SMS from an unlisted phone, etc.

The message came under the dark side's radar, so the identity of the sender is a mystery. (It's the Herald).

Also, after the message is delivered it disappears.

Examples:

Star Wars: Leia's hologram says, "You are my only hope." We don't know who she is. The hologram disappears, and R2D2 pretends not to know how to replay it.

The Matrix: Neo's computer reads, "Follow the White Rabbit." We don't know who's on the other side. "Knock-knock, Neo," says on the screen. And then it goes blank.

Harry Potter: Harry receives a letter, but we don't know from whom. Dudley grabs it from Harry's hands, and Uncle Vernon destroys it.

Sideways: Miles checks his answering machine. "You have no messages."

Dodgeball: An instructional video explains how to play dodgeball, starring the sport's old glory, Patches O'Houlihan. The video ends, and the image disappears from the wall.

Related:
038 – The Herald

038 – The Herald

This character delivers another message, and then vanishes.

Description:

Heralds are both messengers and guides. They leave clues for the Hero to find the path.

This time the communication is personal, but after delivering the message, the Herald goes away.

Examples:

Star Wars: After playing the partial holo-message, R2D2 disappears: He leaves looking for Obi-Wan Kenobi.

The Matrix: In the nightclub, Trinity delivers Neo a message, which guides him to Morpheus. Then she disappears.

Harry Potter: Hagrid delivers the invitation letter, which leads to Dumbledore, and guides Harry to Diagon Alley and Platform 9 ¾. Hagrid then disappears from the train station.

Sideways: Christine's mother gives Miles information, which leads to Jack, and guides him into the house. She disappears from the scene (even if she is still there).

Dodgeball: Jason brings a video, which leads to Patches O'Houlihan, and disappears from the scene (even if he's still there).

Related:
037 – Secret Message
040 – The Herald Returns

039 – Unusual Places
The Adventure World exerts its pull on the Hero.

Description:

The Hero ends up in places closer to the Adventure World. The Hero is not there by chance nor by choice but because the events are already pulling the Hero toward a date with destiny.

This stage is another step in the arc of separation from the Surrogate Parents.

Examples:

Star Wars: Despite the warnings, Luke leaves his uncle's farm and drives deep into the desert, looking for R2D2.

The Matrix: Following Morpheus' instructions, Neo goes to the Adam Street Bridge in the middle of the night, in the middle of the rain.

Harry Potter: Harry finds himself alone at the zoo, talking to a snake.

Sideways: The friends travel among the California vineyards.

Dodgeball: Kate spends less time at Globo Gym and more time with "those freaks over there in Loser Town"—as White Goodman's calls them—despite the villain's warnings to the contrary.

Related:
032 – Resistance to the Separation

040 – The Herald Returns
The Herald shows up again.

Description:

The Herald is not a nanny, nor is there to take the Hero by the hand, but to point the Hero in the right direction. That's why the Herald disappears and reappears all the time.

Examples:

Star Wars: R2D2 reappears; they find him in the rock canyon.

The Matrix: A black car pulls over next to Neo. Trinity tells him to get inside.

Harry Potter: Hagrid reappears; he's waiting at Hogsmeade's train station to guide the kids to the castle.

Sideways: Christine's mother reappears; she suggests that Miles taste the wedding cake samples.

Dodgeball: Young Patches O'Houlihan reappears in the video before it ends, reminding you that "dodgeball is a sport of violence, exclusion and degradation."

Related:
038 – The Herald
042 – The Herald Guides the Hero

041 – Test of Worthiness
The Hero must pass a test before meeting the Mentor.

Description:

The Hero has to prove worthy of the adventure by passing a test, a scan of some sort. But there is another, implicit test: A test of character.

Examples:

Star Wars: The one doing the scanning is Luke; he sees R2D2 in the radar of the speeder. The show of character: Luke orders C3PO to accelerate, despite the dangers that lurk in the desert.

The Matrix: Trinity scans Neo with a scary ultrasound machine, looking for the tracking device the Agents inserted in him. Only when the bug has been removed can Neo meet Morpheus. The test of character: Neo shows that he trusts Trinity—not bad for a guy who believes in nothing.

Harry Potter: First years are scanned by the Sorting Hat. Only when Harry has been assigned to a House can he join his mates. The test of character: Harry shows loyalty to Ron by rejecting Malfoy. Harry's a Gryffindor, indeed.

Sideways: The Erganians "scan" Miles with questions about his delay, about his book, and about his writing. Only when Miles has answered can he depart with the groom.

Dodgeball: A drug-screening test is performed on the Girl Scouts. They fail, so Average Joe's pass to the next round.

Related:
077 – Girl Tests Boy

042 – The Herald Guides the Hero

The Herald fulfills here the role as guide.

Description:

Using some kind of transport, the Herald takes the Hero to the first meeting with the Mentor.

The meeting will happen in a special, secret place. Use the opportunity to create a short but memorable route to this location.

Examples:

***Star Wars*:** C3PO drives the speeder to the lost canyon where the meeting with Obi-Wan will happen.

***The Matrix*:** Trinity and other two members of the crew take Neo to the abandoned building where Morpheus awaits. They move in an awesome 1965 Lincoln Continental.

***Harry Potter*:** A fabulous, antique train takes Harry to his destination: Hogwarts School of Witchcraft and Wizardry.

***Sideways*:** The friends make it into the road in Miles's old Saab.

***Dodgeball*:** A group of young men pushes Peter's old car to the gym. This is not much of a secret place, nor a memorable ride.

Related:
037 – Secret Message

043 – The Hero Is a Mess

The Hero arrives at the meeting not in the best shape.

Description:

The Hero is already in the descending part of the character's arc and arrives at the meeting a little shaken after some rough experience.

Examples:

Star Wars: Luke gets attacked and hurt by the Sand People. Ben Kenobi finds Luke unconscious.

The Matrix: Neo experiences the traumatic extraction of the bug from his abdomen.

Harry Potter: In *The Chamber of Secrets*, Hagrid finds Harry, who was lost. "You're a mess, Harry. Skulking around Knockturn Alley? Dodgy place."

Sideways: Miles is still suffering the effects of the previous night's wine tasting. Jack notices and says, "You're fucking hungover."

Dodgeball: The team is indeed a mess: At the restaurant, White Goodman throws a tray full of Mexican food over them.

044 – Transmogrifications
The Hero starts on a life-changing path.

Description:

During the Journey, the Hero gets bruised, hurt, cut, or wounded in some other way.

These physical ailments are a representation of the change the Hero is undergoing and a foreshadow of the upcoming ultimate sacrifice. The process is called "transmogrification," and blood is a powerful symbol of it.

Examples:

Star Wars: Luke gets knocked unconscious by the Sand People. There is no blood, but later on he's hit by the electrical shocks of the training drone ball, his hand is cut off by Vader, and more.

The Matrix: Neo suffers the traumatic experience of being taken out of the goo pod; they remove the metallic connectors from his body; his mouth gets bloody when he fails the jump simulation, etc.

Harry Potter: In *The Half Blood Prince,* the second act starts with Harry entering the Hogwarts Great Hall. Ginny Weasley says, "He's covered in blood again. Why is he always covered in blood?"

Sideways: There is only one physical wound in the story, which happens later: Stephanie breaks Jack's nose.

Dodgeball: The guys get hurt in very creative ways, usually involving things thrown at them. There is no blood, but there's no scarcity of pain.

Related:

065 – New Clothes
066 – Transitions
068 – Guardians

045 – The Herald's Gift

The Herald either gives the Hero a special object or some important piece of information.

Description:

Heralds are dedicated guardians of the light side. If your story has a Traitor, don't make it a herald. In The Matrix, for example, three people lead Neo to Morpheus, but Cypher, the traitor, is not among them.

The Herald arrives at the last step of his or her mission: To leave the Hero at the doorstep of the Mentor. This event's significance is marked by a gift that the Herald presents to the Hero. This gift can either be an object or a piece of advice, wisdom, or information.

Examples:

Star Wars: R2D2 projects the full holographic message in front of Luke.

The Matrix: Trinity gives Neo a piece of advice regarding Morpheus: "Be honest. He knows more than you can imagine."

Harry Potter: In Diagon Alley, Hagrid brings Harry a new loyal friend: Hedwig, the owl.

Sideways: Christine's mother, acting as herald, gives Miles the cake samples.

Dodgeball: Peter, acting as herald, presents Kate with two expired movie passes and a coupon for "One free back-rub from Peter La Fleur."

Related:
100 – Presentation of Gifts

046 – The Mentor

The arrival of the Mentor scares minor enemies away.

Description:

This stage shows the intimidating power the Mentor has on the dark side. The Mentor's arrival saves the Hero somehow and creates a bond between them.

Examples:

Star Wars: Obi-Wan shows up walking down the canyon, and the Sand People run away in fear.

The Matrix: Morpheus and Neo meet in an abandoned building. The attitude of Morpheus's crew toward their leader is one of utmost respect.

Harry Potter: In *The Chamber of Secrets*, Hagrid, who is the first mentor of Harry, shows up in Knockturn Alley. The dark figures that were converging on the kid backtrack in fear and go away.

Sideways: Miles and Jack meet in the Erganians' living room. They both act as each other's Mentor; no dark figures are scared away here, though.

Dodgeball: Patches, a homophobic, misogynistic old man in a motorized wheelchair enters the gym, takes a deep breath, and says, "Oh, I love the smell of queef in the morning." Everyone looks at him in disbelief. The feeling turns to fear when Patches screams at the guys, "Line up, ladies!"

Related:

047 – Quick Introductions

047 – Quick Introductions

The Mentor is introduced. There is not much time, though.

Description:

Mentor and Hero introduce to each other and move to some other. Because there is danger approaching, lack of privacy, or some time constraint, they have to move somewhere else. Only when they arrive to that new location can the Call to Adventure happen.

Before the conversation takes place, the Herald leaves the scene.

Examples:

Star Wars: Ben Kenobi introduces himself as Obi-Wan, a name he hasn't used in a long time. They have to leave the canyon; the Sand People will return in bigger numbers. Once in the cave, C3PO asks for permission to close down for a while.

The Matrix: Morpheus introduces himself. He tells Neo, "I don't know if you are ready to see what I want to show you, but sadly you and I have run out of time." Trinity leaves.

Harry Potter: Harry arrives at the Grand Hall. Professor Dumbledore presides. Hagrid left the scene.

Sideways: Jack protests the cake tasting. "Don't bother him with that," Jack says. "We've got to get going."

Dodgeball: Patches O'Houlihan introduces himself to Peter as his new coach. They are alone in the alley behind the restaurant. The dialogue lasts a few seconds.

Related:

046 – The Mentor

048 – Historic Battle

The Hero is told the story of the dark side's rise to power.

Description:

The Mentor narrates past events to the Hero, related to the rise of the dark side and its influence in the current state of affairs.

In movies, this stage is an opportunity for interesting visual detours —*The Lord of the Rings* style. In novels this is backstory, which could keep the main story from moving forward. Don't stay too long on it.

Important: The Mentor doesn't disclose everything. If he did, the Hero wouldn't accept the Call to Adventure (stage 052).

Examples:

Star Wars: Obi-Wan tells Luke that his father was actually a Jedi, killed by Vader. Obi-Wan is leaving out a small detail, of course: Vader *is* Luke's father.

The Matrix: This example replaces trauma with mystery. Like Jesus, Neo doesn't have a human biological father (not one we can see, anyway).

Harry Potter: Hagrid tells Harry how his parents died: Killed by Lord Voldemort. The actual truth (Snape's role and Lily's sacrifice) is the ultimate reveal of the story.

Sideways: (Not applicable).

Dodgeball: (Not applicable).

Related:

009 – Mutual Creation
025 – The Hero's Ghost

049 – The Prophecy Is Shared

A prophecy predicted the rise of evil and the coming of the One.

Description:

The prophecy is transmitted only orally, to preserve its secrecy. If it were common knowledge, neutralizing the Hero would be too easy.

Ideal places to share prophecies are dark, arcane, and solitary places, like a cavern, the basement of a castle, an old church, or an abandoned tower.

Examples:

Star Wars: The dialogue takes place in Obi-Wan's cave. He doesn't talk about the prophecy, though, because it refers to Anakin, not to Luke.

The Matrix: Morpheus tells Neo about the prophecy in the privacy of Neo's cabin, deep in the Nebuchadnezzar.

Harry Potter: The prophecy was made by professor Trelawney, and the only person she shared it with was Albus Dumbledore. She said: "The one with the power to vanquish the Dark Lord will be born as the seventh month dies..." (This is part of the novel *Harry Potter and The Order of the Phoenix*, not the movie).

Sideways: Miles predicts, "I'm going to show you a good time. We're going to drink a lot of good wine, play some golf, and send you off in style."

Dodgeball: In Peter's opinion, if his wreck of a car starts in the morning, that's a good enough omen for the day (see 031 – A Storm Is Coming).

Related:

010 – The Sign of the One
050 – The Prophecy Is Incomplete

050 – The Prophecy Is Incomplete
The book of destiny has a few blank pages, waiting to be written.

Description:

The future *has* to be unpredictable; otherwise the concept of freedom wouldn't be possible. This implies that all prophecies are necessarily incomplete.

Don't reveal it yet, but anticipate that because the prophecy is transmitted orally, something is either missing from it, or something was lost in translation, just like in the "telephone" game we used to play when we were kids, remember?

Examples:

Star Wars: Yes, Anakin/Vader brought balance to the Force. But he did it in a rather catastrophic way. Not even Yoda saw that coming.

The Matrix: Yes, Neo is The One. But the prophecy said nothing about the other, previous "Ones"—Neo is the sixth.

Harry Potter is mentioned in a prophecy that anticipates his birth and his death. The good news is that the future has yet to be written.

Sideways: Miles's prophecy was incomplete: They will find much more than golf and wine in this trip.

Dodgeball: Despite Peter's good feelings about the day, it ends up being a disaster.

Related:
049 – The Prophecy Is Shared

051 – Be Careful What You Wish For
Someone's wish comes true (to that character's dismay).

Description:

This stage foreshadows calamities to come.

The Hero wishes for something he believes will help achieve the Goal (stage 022), but he ignores that getting the wish will create other problems.

Examples:

Star Wars: Luke says, "I wish I'd know him," in reference to his father. Oh, Luke, you will.

The Matrix: "I believe that you wish to do the right thing, Mr. Anderson," says Smith. Neo does wish that, which spells calamities for both of them.

Harry Potter: "Make a wish, Harry," he tells himself. He blows the imaginary candles of a cake he drew in the dirt. One second later, the door falls to the floor and Hagrid enters the place where the Dursleys keep Harry hidden. Harry's destiny is set in motion.

Sideways: Jack's wants to get laid before the wedding. His wish comes true (twice), and the consequences include a broken nose and one angry husband running after him.

Dodgeball: "Come on, show of hands. Who wants to play dodgeball?" All of Peter's friends do. All righty then: May the pain begin.

Related:
022 – The Hero's Goal

052 – Call to Adventure
The Mentor asks the Hero to go on the Adventure.

Description:

The Call to Adventure is an encouragement to leave the Ordinary World and to fulfill one's destiny.

The Call happens on some special day: A festivity, an anniversary, a birthday, a sunny day, or a stormy day.

The Call is made in general terms, not yet as a personal appeal.

Examples:

Star Wars: It is another sunny day in Tatooine, a planet with two suns. Obi-Wan asks Luke to go with him to take R2D2 to Alderaan.

The Matrix: The memorable Blue Pill versus Red Pill scene: "You take the red pill, you stay in Wonderland. And I show you how deep the rabbit hole goes."

Harry Potter: Hagrid arrives precisely the minute Harry turns eleven. Hagrid says, "Oh, we're a bit behind schedule. Best be off," inviting Harry to go with him.

Sideways: The special day is arriving: Jack's wedding. Maya, a waitress, comes out from the restaurant's kitchen carrying dishes. Jack says, "You know that chick? She is very hot."

Dodgeball: It's not Peter's birthday until next month, which adds to the comedic effect, because, who cares? Also, there's no proper Call to Adventure here; Patches just informs Peter that he's the new coach.

Related:

053 – First Refusal of the Call
055 – The Mentor's Rebuttal
057 – Second Refusal of the Call
062 – Answer to the Call

053 – First Refusal of the Call
The Hero can't do it—just can't. I swear.

Description:

The Hero's resists leaving the Ordinary World, offering some reasonable but mundane excuse, which is connected to the Hero's Lie. That excuse will soon be rendered irrelevant by the events that will ensue.

Examples:

Star Wars: "I can't get involved," Luke says. "I've got work to do. It's not that I like the Empire. I hate it! But there's nothing I can do about it right now."

The Matrix: Switch tells Neo to do as they say or to go away. Neo says "Okay," and he motions to leave the car.

Harry Potter: Harry's Refusal of the Call takes a subtle form: He stops for just a second to ponder if he should follow Hagrid or not.

Sideways: Miles refuses approaching Maya. She's very hot, "and very nice, and very married to some professor. Check out the rock," he says in reference to her promise ring.

Dodgeball: Peter dismisses Patches, "Okay, crazy guy. I'm gonna go home now."

Bonus Example:

In some stories with willing heroes, sometimes the Mentor is the one refusing the call. In *The Empire Strikes Back*, Yoda resists training Luke. In *The Karate Kid* (1984), Mr. Miyagi initially resists training Daniel.

Related:

052 – Call to Adventure
054 – Our Most Desperate Hour
055 – The Mentor's Rebuttal
057 – Second Refusal of the Call

054 – Our Most Desperate Hour

It is now or never.

Description:

This is not just another mission. This is vital to save the world as we know it ("the world" being an entire galaxy or Jack's last days as a bachelor).

The Mentor transmits the seriousness of the situation, including a warning about this being the last chance to start the Adventure.

Examples:

Star Wars: Leia's hologram says, "This is our most desperate hour. Help me, Obi-Wan Kenobi."

The Matrix: Morpheus tells Neo, "No one can be told what the Matrix is. You have to see it for yourself. This is your last chance."

Harry Potter: Voldemort's return is discussed in dialogues that, for at least another two movies of the series, don't include Harry. But it is clear that the magic world will soon face its darker hours.

Sideways: Jack tells Miles, "This is our last chance. This is our week!"

Dodgeball: Peter says, "This place is in default?" Kate answers, "No. You're in foreclosure. You were in default when the bank sent you delinquency notices."

Related:

052 – Call to Adventure
053 – First Refusal of the Call
055 – The Mentor's Rebuttal
057 – Second Refusal of the Call

055 – The Mentor's Rebuttal
The Mentor tries to change the Hero's mind.

Description:

The Call to Adventure is a challenge to face one's innermost fears—a call to meet one's destiny.

This Mentor's rebuttal doesn't work: The Hero persists in making excuses.

Examples:

Star Wars: Obi-Wan says, "I need your help, Luke. I'm getting too old for this sort of thing." Luke refuses again.

The Matrix: (Not applicable).

Harry Potter: Harry's hesitation to go with him causes Hagrid to say, "Best be off. Unless you'd rather stay, of course. Hm?"

Sideways: Jack says, "So what's a professor's wife doing waitressing? Obviously that's over." Miles dismisses him again. He just wants to have dinner, drink wine, and go back to the hotel.

Dodgeball: Patches says, "I ain't crazy and I ain't a guy. The name's Patches O'Houlihan. And I'm your new coach."

Related:

052 – Call to Adventure
053 – First Refusal of the Call
054 – Our Most Desperate Hour
057 – Second Refusal of the Call

056 – Presentation of the Sword

The Hero receives a weapon to help in the quest.

Description:

The Hero is a warrior, and a warrior needs a weapon.

The Sword doesn't have to be an actual sword; sometimes it's not even a material object. Controlling the Sword means taking a quantum leap above the ordinary self. The Hero has a bumpy start but soon learns how to control the newly acquired weapon or ability.

This Sword will be replaced by a more powerful weapon later on.

Examples:

Star Wars: Luke receives his father's lightsaber from Obi-Wan. He loves it. He learns to use it, though he gets zapped a few times in the process. Soon he is blocking the electric shots from the drone.

The Matrix: Neo gets martial arts knowledge uploaded to his brain. He loves it. He shows Morpheus what he learned, and he gets his butt kicked in the process. But in a matter of minutes, he learns the rules of the game and surpasses his teacher.

Harry Potter: Harry receives the invisibility cloak from an anonymous person (Dumbledore). He loves it. He uses it to enter the library's restricted section. His presence is discovered, but he manages to escape from Filch and Snape.

Sideways: Jack tells Miles about his gift as best man: Not a foldable knife, but sex. "I prefer a knife," Miles says. He ends up enjoying the romantic night spent with Maya, though.

Dodgeball: Peter receives Patches's stained scarf, a symbol of delegation of leadership. He eventually uses it to win the final match.

Related:

146 – Sword Upgrade
173 – Emergence of the Sword

057 – Second Refusal of the Call
"Sorry, I have to go."

Description:

The Hero refuses the Call once again, and leaves.

Home is the classic symbol of the Ordinary World, and the Hero is clinging to it. There is something the Hero ignores, though: If this denial persists, tragedy will take over and there will be no home left to return to.

Examples:

Star Wars: Luke refuses again to go to Alderaan. He leaves Obi-Wan's cave and heads home. But the farm is gone, as he will soon find out.

The Matrix: Neo refuses to believe what he was just told: The world as he knows it only exists as a simulation, which they call The Matrix. "Let me out!," he screams. "Let me out. I want out!" But there is no home to return to: Everything is an illusion.

Harry Potter: (Not applicable).

Sideways: After this trip, all that's waiting for Miles is the tedium of his ordinary, solitary life.

Dodgeball: This example is different in that the Ultimate Boon is to save the only place where they feel at home.

Related:

052 – Call to Adventure
053 – First Refusal of the Call
054 – Our Most Desperate Hour
055 – The Mentor's Rebuttal

058 – The Mentor's Warning

The Mentor warns the Hero against ignoring the sage's advice.

Description:

The Mentor's warning is intended to help the Hero avoid danger. But if the Hero wasn't drawn to danger he or she would be living a quiet life.

So the Hero disobeys the warning, of course, and pays a price for it.

Examples:

Star Wars: Ben warns Luke against returning to the farm: "No! Wait Luke! It's too dangerous!" Luke ignores him and runs away. He risks getting killed by the Empire.

The Matrix: Morpheus warns Neo that the Agents are at his office in order to take him into custody. Morpheus tries to guide Neo to escape by taking a scaffold to the roof. Neo doesn't follow the instructions and he gets arrested.

Harry Potter: Dumbledore warns the students: The third floor corridor on the right hand side is out of bounds to everyone who does not wish to die a most painful death. There is precisely where Harry, Ron, and Hermione end up going.

Sideways: Miles tells Jack not to open the 1992 Byron. Jack does it anyway. "For Christ's Sake, Jack! You just wasted like half of it!"

Dodgeball: Jason insists on going beyond his limits on the pull-down machine. "All that weight is dangerous," Peter warns. But it's too late: The kid is entangled with steel cables.

Related:
016 – The Mentor's Knowledge

059 – Pushing Event

Something shocking happens. The only option is to go forward.

Description:

The problem has reached the Hero; it has affected (or destroyed) life as the Hero knows it, and there is no safe place left to retreat.

Examples:

Star Wars: The farm is destroyed; Luke's uncle and aunt have been murdered. Luke would have been killed, too, had he been there. He is sad, angry, and appalled.

The Matrix: Neo is detained and interrogated by the Agents, who freak him out by literally sealing his mouth. He wakes up in his bed, not knowing what is real anymore.

Harry Potter: Hagrid tells Harry that his parents were killed by Voldemort.

Sideways: Jack tells Miles that his ex-wife, Victoria, got re-married.

Dodgeball: The Pushing Event takes a painful shape: Actual wrenches thrown at you. Start moving or suffer.

Bonus Examples:

Armageddon: Small meteorites damage several cities. The Big One is coming.

World War Z: A zombie outbreak starts.

Independence Day (1996): Immense flying saucers have stationed directly above the main cities of the world.

Related:
029 – The Inciting Event

060 – No Appeal Possible
There is no one to go crying for help to.

Description:

Authorities are either unavailable or impotent. Uncle died; dad left for work; the king is under a spell; the President has been kidnapped; the Emperor has lost his mind, etc.

If the crisis can be averted by issuing an executive order, then why write a novel about it, right?

Examples:

Star Wars: Luke has nobody. He cannot stay on the farm, because the stormtroopers can return any time.

The Matrix: Neo has no one. And the authorities are after him.

Harry Potter: Harry is alone in the world because the Dursleys are not his family, really.

Sideways: Miles lives alone, divorced with no children.

Dodgeball: Peter lives alone, and the gym is everything he has left—not that he cares much, though.

Related:
116 – The Mentor Is Gone

061 – First Epiphany

*Revelation: **The Hero is part of the problem.***

Description:

The First Epiphany happens when the Hero realizes that this is personal. The Hero is both a victim and a solution for the problem posed by the dark side.

After acquiring this knowledge, or after the terrible Pushing Event (stage 059), the Hero cannot keep refusing the Call.

Note that this stage and the next one (062 - Answer to the Call) mark the ending of Act 1.

Examples:

Star Wars: For all Luke knows, the Empire killed his father, and now they've also killed the rest of his family. How more personal can it get?

The Matrix: Neo finally accepts that he was a prisoner in the Matrix, and that a war against the Machines is going on.

Harry Potter: Harry learns that he is the only person who ever survived an attack by Voldemort. He starts realizing the connection between him and the Dark Lord.

Sideways: The news about his ex-wife's new marriage throws Miles into a mild panic attack. He runs down a hill, into some vineyards, and drinks a full bottle of wine. Jack contains him.

Dodgeball: It has been personal from the beginning: The gym is their home.

Related:
119 – Second Epiphany

062 – Answer to the Call
The Hero finally accepts the challenge.

Description:

The Answer has to be explicit: The Hero either says the words ("I'll do it") or takes an action that denotes acceptance of the challenge.

The next sentence you write after this scene will be already in Act 2. Consider emphasizing that fact by ending a chapter here.

Examples:

Star Wars: Luke tells Obi-Wan, "I want to come with you to Alderaan."

The Matrix: Neo swallows the red pill.

Harry Potter: Harry goes with Hagrid. He never looks back.

Sideways: Before they go into the restaurant, Jack tells Miles not to go to the dark side (in those very words). Miles reluctantly agrees. In the movie script he takes a pill, too—an anxiolytic.

Dodgeball: Peter admits to the guys that he accepted Patches as coach. Oh, my.

Related:
052 – Call to Adventure

063 – The Hero is Welcome
The Hero arrives at the Adventure World.

Description:

Just as Jesus was hailed by the Three Kings, the Hero is greeted as he steps into a new world, too. The party doing the welcome is small: The Hero is just coming out of anonymity.

This is usually the first time we get to see the character that later on will be revealed as the Traitor.

Examples:

Star Wars: Luke and Obi-Wan enter the Cantina. They are welcome; the droids aren't. A spy observes their movements.

The Matrix: Neo is introduced and welcome by the crew, including Cypher.

Harry Potter: Harry is greeted at the Leaky Cauldron by the patrons, including Quirrell.

Sideways: Miles is greeted as he arrives at the home of the Erganians (Miles is a self-sabotaging character, so there's no need for a Traitor here).

Dodgeball: Peter La Fleur is greeted by everyone when he arrives at the Gym. (Peter's story is one of self-sabotage, too).

Related:
074 – The Traitor
096 – The Hero Is Recognized

ACT 2.1

064 – Plan A: Let Events Unfold
The only plan is to go forward—for now.

Description:

The mission of the Mentor is to enlist the Hero, put the Hero on the right path, and help for as long as possible.

Tactical decisions are left to the Hero, whose head at this point is still spinning.

A plan will take shape in the Hero's mind as the story unfolds; right now, the Hero's actions are reactive, because the Hero doesn't know what the Villain's game is.

Examples:

Star Wars: The only plan Obi-Wan has is taking R2D2 to Alderaan so they can extract the plans of the Death Star from his memory.

The Matrix: There is no plan, actually. Morpheus doesn't seem to be planning ahead. He just trusts the prophecy and wants to prepare Neo for his destiny. "What was said was for you and for you alone," he says when they leave the Oracle's apartment.

Harry Potter: There is no explicit plan, yet. Dumbledore just wants to prepare Harry for his destiny. "Let the events unfold," says Snape.

Sideways: There's no plan but to have fun. Jack says, "We should both be cutting loose."

Dodgeball: Peter says, "What do you guys want from me? I don't have a plan for you."

Related:
120 – Plan B: Rescue
143 – Plan C: Infiltrate

065 – New Clothes

The Hero's external aspect changes as the quest progresses.

Description:

The Hero changes into a uniform, a disguise, or into different clothes. The changes aren't merely stylistic, of course, but dictated by the circumstances. The external change is a metaphor of inner change.

Examples:

Star Wars: Luke leaves his farmer outfit behind. He dresses like a stormtrooper to infiltrate the Death Star, like a pilot for combat, like an elegant citizen in the award ceremony, and like a Jedi.

The Matrix: Neo starts dressed in regular street clothes; then we see him in a suit and tie, naked inside the goo pod, dressed as a crewman, and finally sporting a lot of ultra-cool, Issey Miyaki-style outfits. Dressing well is cheap when the clothes are virtual, isn't it?

Harry Potter: Harry first changes into his Hogwarts' robes. Then he dresses like a Quidditch player and like a Gryffindor, with the red-and-yellow scarf. Oh, and he uses an invisibility cloak to infiltrate the library.

Sideways: Miles starts in his underwear, awaken by his landlord. Then he dresses like a regular guy, like a high-school professor in a suit and tie, and like a golfer; he wears a swimsuit, a tuxedo in the wedding, and finally a lively colored shirt as he heads to Maya's house.

Dodgeball: Peter La Fleur also starts in his underwear. Then we see him in regular clothes, in a sadomasochist outfit, and finally wearing the glorious yellow uniform. The most dramatic change in appearance is that of Steve, though, once he overcomes his psychotic delusion about being a pirate.

Related:

146 – Suit Up

066 – Transitions

Mentor and Hero cross the border into the Adventure World.

Description:

Sometimes the Hero stops at the physical border before taking the first step into the new world, but adapts quickly: The Adventure World is the place where the Hero will shine.

Along the way, the Hero finds new friends, guardians, enemies, and maybe love, too.

Examples:

Star Wars: Ben and Luke travel across space aboard the Millennium Falcon; they make friends with Han and Chewbacca, and they play holographic chess.

The Matrix: Neo travels aboard the Nebuchadnezzar. There he rests, is healed, officially meets the crew, and reencounters Trinity.

Harry Potter: Harry travels aboard the Hogwarts Express, where he meets Ron and Hermione. Also, there are plenty of sweets and magic tricks (*"Oculus Reparo!"*).

Sideways: Miles and Jack travel aboard an old Saab convertible through Santa Barbara County, tasting great wines and great food. They meet Stephanie and Maya.

Dodgeball: The team leaves for Las Vegas. There, Justin meets Amber, and Owen approaches Fran.

Related:
044 – Transmogrifications

067 – The Team Is Assembled

The good guys are on the road to the adventure.

Description:

We see the good guys team as it is now (except sometimes for the Goddess, who in many stories still has to join the team).

They are on the road to adventure, so usually the team is first assembled on board some vehicle.

Examples:

Star Wars: The team is assembled for the first time on board the Millennium Falcon: Ben, Luke, Han, Chewie, R2D2, C3PO. Leia is not yet in scene.

The Matrix: The team is assembled for the first time on board the Nebuchadnezzar. Trinity is there, but until now she only fulfilled the role of Herald, not yet the role of Goddess. The other Goddess, the Oracle, is not yet in scene.

Harry Potter: The team is assembled for the first time on board the Hogwarts' Express: Harry, Ron, and Hermione (she's Ron's Goddess). Harry's Goddesses, who are Ginny Weasley and Professor McGonagall, are not yet in scene.

Sideways: The team of two friends is assembled for the first time on board the old Saab. Maya is not yet in scene.

Dodgeball: The team is assembled for the first time at the Gym: Peter, Jason, Gordon, and the others. Kate is there, but she still has to accept to be in the team—i.e., stepping into the role of Goddess.

Related:
076 – First Encounter with the Goddess

068 – Guardians

Each time the Hero wants to cross a border,
a Guardian makes it difficult.

Description:

Guardians make great obstacles and conflict creators, because they are the custodians of valuable things and important places.

Never make it easy for anyone to enter or to leave a new place. Guardians offer the chance for Heros to show their talents, for the allies to show their loyalties, and for the Villains to show their powers.

Examples:

Star Wars: It seems that entering into places in that universe is easy; leaving those places is the problem, as seen in the detention area, the sewer, the Death Star, etc.

The Matrix: This simulated world is full of guardians: Machines, Agents, SWAT teams, policemen, passwords, sentient software, etc.

Harry Potter: In contrast to *Star Wars*, pretty much all places in *Harry Potter* are difficult to get into: Diagon Alley, Gringotts Bank, Hogwarts, secret chambers, hidden rooms, and a lot more.

Sideways: Most Guardians here work in the gastronomic industry: Restaurant hostesses, bartenders, servers, wine tasting personnel, etc.

Dodgeball: At Average Joe's, the guardian is a deranged young man who thinks he is a pirate: He puts a knife on Peter's throat to ascertain his identity before letting him through.

Related:
044 – Transmogrifications
066 – Transitions

069 – Presentation of the Elixir
The Hero is given a life-saving resource.

Description:

The Elixir is something almost mundane, but miraculous. It is an object that later on (in stage 166) will allow the Hero's Resurrection.

This scene is short: The Hero receives the thing, puts it in a pocket, and both the Hero and the audience forget about it.

In all James Bond movies, "Q" gives 007 the gizmos he uses in his missions. It used to be a Rolex or an Omega watch equipped with a laser beam, or things like that. But in *Skyfall* (2012), it's just a radio locator; a little button that saves James from certain death.

Examples:

Star Wars: This Elixir is rather large: The Millennium Falcon. It is described as a "piece of junk," but it will blast Vader's TIE Fighter out of the sky.

The Matrix: This Elixir is, fittingly to the premise of the movie, something immaterial: The prediction the Oracle made to Trinity (about Trinity falling in love with The One).

Harry Potter: In *Harry Potter and The Deathly Hallows*, Harry receives the Golden Snitch (a small, winged Quidditch ball) that Dumbledore left for him. Is this just a memento from the old wizard? Sure. But the Resurrection Stone is hidden inside.

Sideways: Miles's Elixir is his answering machine. A life-changing message is recorded in there, waiting for Miles to press that button.

Dodgeball: Gordon always takes his copy of the official ADAA Dodgeball Rule Book with him. That little object will save the friends once and again.

Related:
165 – Emergence of the Elixir

070 – Baptism of Water

Water (real or symbolic) washes the past away.

Description:

Unlike the Baptism of Fire (stage 093), this baptism is only ritual—not a fight, but a rebirth.

Make it subliminal if you must, but include some water symbolism, if possible in the form of a bath: The Hero is reborn from it.

Examples:

Star Wars: Tatooine is a desert planet—there's not much water there. But C3PO is submerged in a bath of oil and reemerges as Luke's inseparable companion.

The Matrix: When Neo is unplugged from the Matrix he emerges from a liquid substance (reminiscent of amniotic liquid), contained in a pod reminiscent of a uterus. Then he falls in water, sinks, and reemerges from it as a free man in the real world.

Harry Potter: Harry sails from Hogsmeade to Hogwarts; he arrives at the other side of the water as a Hogwarts student.

Sideways: Ships are christened with a bottle of champagne; here Jack opens one to celebrate and spills the liquid all over the car and over themselves.

Dodgeball: The Heroes start the adventure setting up a car wash. They end up soaked and with just one, crazy customer ("That's it, boy. Get in there nice and deep, like."). The enterprise fails, but they are a team now.

Related:

093 – Baptism of Fire: Failure
094 – Baptism of Fire: Rescue

071 – Down the Rabbit Hole
Before going up, everything must go down.

Description:

The protagonists either fall into a literal hole (sewers are a recurring motif) or a figurative one (i.e., a situation that sucks). At the very least, the words "hole" or "hell" are used as a metaphor.

Sometimes the Hero falls together with an ally, and some other ally rescues them. However, the Mentor is out of this scene: The Mentor doesn't fall, nor is the Mentor the one that rescues the Hero.

Examples:

Star Wars: Luke and friends escape through a hole and end up falling into a sewer-like garbage compactor with moving walls. They are rescued by C3PO and R2D2.

The Matrix: During the Call to Adventure, Morpheus said, "I imagine that right now you're feeling a bit like Alice, tumbling down the rabbit hole." Later on, Neo falls through an actual hole, through a tube, and into a sewer. He is rescued by Tank and Dozer.

Harry Potter: In *The Chamber of Secrets*, Harry, Ron, and Lockhart jump into a hole, down into the castle's plumbing system. They are rescued by Fawkes, the phoenix. Harry will also fall into Aragog's cave, through the Devil's Snare, and a few other holes, yet.

Sideways: Miles and Jack run down a hill and end up by the vines at the bottom of it. Miles's depression is a symbolic hole, too.

Dodgeball: It seems that there are no options left for the team of friends. Peter says, "We gave it a hell of a run, guys." (Note the mention of hell). Then Gordon saves the day: He reads about a dodgeball tournament in Las Vegas, in his copy of Obscure Sports Quarterly.

Related Stage:
138 – No Way Back, No Way Forward

# 072 – No Going Back

Just like life, good stories don't have an "undo" button.

Description:

The Hero is determined to continue. But even if the Hero weren't, going back is out of the question. The Heroes suspect that the Adventure might hurt but know that the decadence of the Ordinary World will kill them.

Well, adventure may kill them, too.

Examples:

Star Wars: Obi-Wan tells Luke that he will have to sell his speeder to pay Han for the trip to Alderaan. Luke says, "That's okay. I'm never coming back to this planet again."

The Matrix: Neo says, "I can't go back, can I?" Morpheus answers, "No. But if you could, would you really want to?" Neo knows he doesn't.

Harry Potter: Harry doesn't express any regrets; on the contrary, he is happy to at Hogwarts. From his dorm's window he looks at the moonlight reflected on the bay: He found a home here.

Sideways: Miles and Jack argue. Miles threatens to leave, saying, "Take the car. I'll catch the train back." Jack refuses, of course—nobody is going back anywhere.

Dodgeball: The guys put the idea of playing dodgeball to a vote. They are all in. (Dwight's proposal of selling blood and semen was rejected.) Peter has no option but joining them. "You guys had me at blood and semen," he says

Related:

082 – Stakes Increase
138 – No Way Back, No Way Forward

073 – The Hero's Determination
The Hero shows readiness to advance.

Description:

This stage comprises one simple expression of agreement or readiness. It shows the Hero's well-intended immaturity, because he underestimates the challenges ahead.

Examples:

Star Wars: Obi-Wan warns Luke before entering the cantina, "Watch your step. This place can be a little rough." Luke says, "I'm ready for anything".

The Matrix: Neo just got Jiu-Jitsu uploaded to his brain. Tank asks him if he wants some more; Neo says, "Oh, yes. Hell, yeah."

Harry Potter: Determination is Harry's signature trait. He shows it, for example, by running directly toward a wall between platforms 9 and 10 at King's Cross Station.

Sideways: Miles tells Jack, "Despite your crass behavior, I'm really glad we're finally getting this time together."

Dodgeball: See stage 072.

Related:
172 – The Hero's Verbal Attack

074 – The Traitor

Someone follows the Hero's movements.

Description:

The Traitor's role is to create conflict, which is vital in order to move the story forward.

Note that the Traitor doesn't directly works against the Hero, because the Traitor failed to assess the threat the Hero implies, just as the Villain did. The Traitor works for the dark side, but it's ultimately for some personal benefit: Money, revenge, freedom.

The Traitor is scheming in the shadows, which is difficult to show in a first-person narrative because the point-of-view character supposedly ignores that there is a Traitor. In such cases, all the author can do is plant clues of the Traitor's movements.

Examples:

Star Wars: Ben and Luke try to leave Tatooine. A hooded figure alerts the stormtroopers. They don't even notice the presence of the spy.

The Matrix: Neo approaches Cypher, who is going through his night shift on the ship's bridge. Cypher acts suspiciously and turns off all the monitors. Neo doesn't realize what Cypher is up to (he was coordinating a meeting with the Agents).

Harry Potter: Ron travels with Scabbers, his pet rat, which is actually the Animagus Peter Pettigrew, a traitor, transmogrified.

Sideways: The Traitor in this case is represented by both protagonists and their self-sabotage.

Dodgeball: Peter's Traitor is Peter himself: Self-sabotage again.

Related:
111 – Traitor on the Move

075 – Book of Laws

Some authority figure explains the laws of the Adventure World.

Description:

New worlds have new rules, especially in fantasy, science fiction, and other genres with intensive world building.

Do not fall into long information dumps or backstory. Focus on the way things are *now* in your world, instead. Readers will suspend their disbelief but will not be so tolerant with long explanations. Only discuss rules that affect the plot; the rest is descriptions.

Examples:

Star Wars: Obi-Wan explains, "The Force is what gives a Jedi his power. It's an energy field created by all living things. It surrounds us and penetrates us. It binds the galaxy together." (I had no problem believing this—well, not until they started talking about midiclorians).

The Matrix: Morpheus explains, "These rules are no different that the rules of a computer system. Some of them can be bent. Others can be broken."

Harry Potter: McGonagall explains, "Your triumphs will earn your house points; any rule breaking and you will lose points. At the end of the year, the house with the most points is awarded the House Cup." Questions?

Sideways: Miles explains how to taste a wine: "First take your glass and examine the wine against the light. You're looking at color and clarity." Jack just wants to drink it. And he's chewing gum.

Dodgeball: Patches explains the five *d*'s of Dodgeball: "Dodge, duck, dip, dive, dodge!" Either follow them or bleed. Your call.

Related:

075 – Book of Laws
107 – Breaking the Law

076 – Encounter with the Goddess
*Without her, the Hero doesn't
have a chance in hell.*

Description:

The Hero and the Goddess (i.e. the *ego* and the *anima*, in Jungian terms) start out polarized or divided; they are opposites, after all. But they are also complementary, and they converge as the story evolves.

The Goddess is a driver for the forward movement, an inspiration for the Hero to prove worthy.

"They meet for the first time" means: For the first time in this story or for the first time as potential lovers—not necessarily for the first time ever in their lives.

Examples:

Star Wars: Luke enters the cell where Leia is kept prisoner. This scene plays like an intentional misdirection of the plot regarding romance, because they are actually brother and sister, of course.

The Matrix: Neo enters the kitchen where The Oracle is baking cookies. She is one of the Goddesses in this story; Trinity is the other.

Harry Potter: Hermione enters the train compartment where the boys are. When she leaves, Ron says, "Mental, that one. I'm telling you."

Sideways: Miles enters the restaurant where Maya works. He knew her from before, and they have a nice, short dialogue. There is attraction but nothing else.

Dodgeball: Peter enters his office, where Kate is already working.

Related:
030 – The Goddess

077 – Girl Tests Boy

The girl has to see what her romantic interest is made of.

Description:

Selecting a good partner is the essence of the evolution of most animal species, isn't it?

This test takes the form of a question that the Goddess poses to the Hero, who can't respond adequately.

Also, if there is any romance potential here, our Hero will need another chance to show any seductive powers because this time it resulted in a miserable fail.

Examples:

Star Wars: Princess Leia asks, "Aren't you a little short to be a stormtrooper?" Luke just stands there, not knowing what to say.

The Matrix: The Oracle asks: "So, what do you think? You think you're The One?" Neo doesn't know. Then she says, "Well, I better have a look at you. Open your mouth; say 'ahhh.'" After the test, she lets Neo arrive at the (wrong) conclusion that he's not The One.

Harry Potter: Hermione asks Ron: "Oh, are you doing magic? Let's see then." He tries to turn his rat, Scabbers, yellow. The spell doesn't work.

Sideways: Maya asks, "So how's that book of yours going, Miles? I think you were almost done with it last time we talked." Miles lies about it.

Dodgeball: Kate asks for the gym's financial records; Peter opens a closet and a huge pile of documents falls to the floor. Peter flirts with her to no avail.

Related:
076 – First Encounter with the Goddess

078 – Training: Success
The Hero makes some progress.

Description:

The Hero goes through competitions, initiations, questions, auditions, or anything intended to improve proficiency. The Hero learns fast, but the Weakness will soon be revealed.

Here in Act 2.1, the trials are either part of a training or minor battles; in Act 2.3, the trials become increasingly serious challenges.

Examples:

Star Wars: Luke blocks the electric shocks from the training drone with his lightsaber. He learns fast.

The Matrix: Neo's passes the dojo test. He's even faster than Morpheus.

Harry Potter: Harry wins his first Quidditch match.

Sideways: Miles barely passes the test of establishing conversation with the girls.

Dodgeball: We see Jason getting hit by balls, and—oh, God—wrenches. The rest of the team does pretty well, though.

Related:

026 – The Hero's Weakness
041 – Test of Worthiness
077 – Girl Tests Boy

079 – First Encouragement
The trials become more difficult.

Description:

The road to victory is paved with success. But the road to success is paved with failures. Nonetheless, the Hero receives encouragement before the next challenge.

Examples:

Star Wars: The training gets harder: Luke has to block the shocks blindfolded. He gets zapped. Obi-Wan tells him, "Try again, Luke."

The Matrix: The training gets more difficult: Neo must jump between two buildings. Trinity whispers, "Come on."

Harry Potter: Professor McGonagall is the one who does the encouraging in every movie, in a gentle but sarcastic way. When the kids arrive late at her class, she tells Ron, "If I were to transfigure Mr. Potter or yourself into a pocket watch, maybe one of you would be on time."

Sideways: Miles starts a conversation with Maya about the Fiddleback she is drinking. She encourages him to taste her cup of the sauvignon blanc: "Try it." It is an encouragement to share, a subtle invitation to get closer to each other.

Dodgeball: The guys encourage Gordon: "You got it, Gord." And he runs across the highway. Or he tries, at least.

Related:
141 – Second Encouragement
169 – Third Encouragement

080 – Training: Failure

The Hero fails some harder test.

Description:

Of course the Hero fails; it's because of the Weakness.

This problem persists until stage 142 – Third Epiphany, when the Hero finally realizes what to do with that inner limitation.

Examples:

Star Wars: Luke received a couple of electric shocks from the training drone; his weakness is that he doesn't trust the Force. (He eventually succeeds, though).

The Matrix: Neo fails the jump. His weakness is his disbelief. He is told to leave doubts, fear, and disbelief behind. He can't.

Harry Potter: Professor Snape ridicules Harry in front of the whole class. Harry's weakness is his lack of knowledge about magic.

Sideways: Miles fails to follow Jack's request and ends up drinking too much during the dinner at the restaurant.

Dodgeball: Gordon gets hit by a car. He is okay. Then he gets hit again.

Related:

078 – Training: Success
079 – First Encouragement

ROAD OF TRIALS — The Ultimate Hero's Journey — ACT **2.1**

081 – The False Enemy
Mislead your readers by planting a fake bad guy.

Description:

A traitor is an enemy who looks like a friend; a false enemy is a friend who looks like an enemy. Both characters benefit from subtlety; don't say, "Surely the disgusting Mr. Galveston was behind the fishy business going on," only to reveal that he was a good guy after all.

The False Enemy's true allegiance must be kept unknown to the Hero, to the audience, or to both. A good place for revealing the False Enemy as a good guy is stage 167 – The Cavalry Arrives.

Examples:

Star Wars: Han Solo is a smuggler and a gambler, only interested in money. He doesn't care about the Empire or the Rebellion. Predictability: Han is too handsome, fun, and charming to be a real enemy.

The Matrix: The misdirection comes from the one who's supposed to tell the truth: The Oracle. She lets Neo think he's not The One. But that's exactly what he needed. Predictability: None. We all fell for it.

Harry Potter: Professor Snape is the False Enemy, acting as a double agent. He is actually a good guy, of course, acting out of loyalty to Dumbledore and of love for Harry's mother, Lily. Classic.

Sideways: Here things are never as simple as in the other examples. Both Miles and Jack are the Hero, the Villain, the Mentor, and the False Enemy—all at the same time. Such human complexity is what makes this movie great (it was nominated for five Oscars).

Dodgeball: As a comedy, this example remains pretty simple in this regard: No red herrings here—just a hysterical Villain. The objective is to induce laughter, not to build a suspenseful masterpiece.

Related:
167 – The Cavalry Arrives

082 – Stakes Increase
We get another peek into what's really at play.

Description:

The author's job is to involve the audience more and more in the story, and this is done by raising the importance of what's at stake. Otherwise, the adventure becomes a devalued enterprise.

Consider not only the external stakes (the ones described in the examples below) but also the inner ones: It is the Hero's *life* that is truly at stake. Well, not necessarily the Hero's actual life, but the Hero's honor, worth, and all that the Hero loves.

Examples:

Star Wars: Luke starts with mere curiosity about the holo-message. Then he fights stormtroopers, rescues a princess, and finally saves a whole planet.

The Matrix: At first, Neo only thinks about saving himself. Then he saves Morpheus, then the Nebuchadnezzar, then Trinity, and finally he must save humanity. It took three movies to go through that arc, though.

Harry Potter: Harry started with a children's rivalry with Malfoy, then he faced all kinds of opponents, and he ended up facing Voldemort in order to save the world.

Sideways: What started as a wine-tasting trip becomes a life-changing experience.

Dodgeball: At first, Average Joe's faced the qualifying match, then it was the championship, and then it was the controlling stake of Globo Gym Corporation. At the end, *Dodgeball* is about honoring friendship.

Related:

072 – No Going Back
138 – No Way Back, No Way Forward

083 – The Random Ally

Some disinterested gesture by the Hero wins a new friend.

Description:

This is good karma in action.

We see the Hero's kindness toward someone who doesn't receive much of that from other people. This circumstantial friend will reappear to help the Hero.

This is a minor character that the Hero met by chance. This character shows up, disappears, and reappears later as The Elixir or The Cavalry—think the Dove Lady in *Home Alone*, 1990.

Note that this character is not the same as the one in stage 144 - The Reluctant Aid.

Examples:

Star Wars: In *Episode VI – The Return of the Jedi*, our heroes are friendly to the Ewoks. When everything seems lost, these furry little things push the Battle of Endor in favor of the Rebellion. They certainly know how to sling a stone.

The Matrix: Neo's Random Ally is Spoon Boy, described in stage 097 – Right Words at the Right Time (1).

Harry Potter: Harry makes lots of odd friends who come to his aid: Dobby the Elf, Buckbeak the Hippogriff, Moaning Myrtle, etc.

Sideways: (Not applicable).

Dodgeball: (Not applicable).

Related:
144 – The Reluctant Aid

084 – Snake Symbolism

The dark side is associated with a symbolic (or real) snake.

Description:

Snakes have represented evil since time immemorial—an archetypical association with the danger they embody. Myth echoes that primal fear by surrounding the figure of the Villain with this symbolism.

If it fits the genre of your story (like fantasy, for example), put at least one snake, serpent, reptile, or dragon in there. If such creatures would look out of place in your story, for example in a romantic comedy, or in a war story happening inside a submarine, then include them anyway, but make it subtle.

Instead of reptiles, some stories include skulls, spiders, ghosts, monsters, vampires, or a legendary creature, like the Golem or Bigfoot.

Examples:

Star Wars: Luke fights a Dianoga slug, a snake-like creature that lurks in the deepest sewer of the Death Star.

The Matrix: Here the snake symbolism is replaced by that of a virus, which is better adapted to computer-centered science fiction.

Harry Potter: The parade of snakes has no end. Voldemort himself looks like a snake, of course. But then we have Slytherin House, Nagini, *Vipera Evanesca*, the Basilisk, dragons, and so forth.

Sideways: Finally, a story that doesn't refer to snakes at all. Jack has to run naked through an ostrich farm, though, which sadly happens off-screen. ("Those fuckers are mean!")

Dodgeball: The Villain's team is called "The Purple Cobras," with a snake in their logo and everything.

Related:

090 – Blindness Symbolism
185 – Consummation of Love

085 – Surpassing Peers

The Hero surpasses the Mentor.
The best of them all, however, is the Goddess.

Description:

Once the Hero has surpassed all peers and Mentors, the only one left to surpass is the Villain, something that right now seems impossible.

But this stage shows the talent of the Hero's counter-sexual figure: The Goddess. She is more intelligent, studious, and resourceful than everyone else—the Hero included.

Examples:

Star Wars: Leia is the only person with more commanding talent than Luke or Obi-Wan. She is the bravest and the most intelligent of them all.

The Matrix: In the dojo simulation, Neo moves faster than Morpheus. The only person with better combat ability than him is Trinity. For now, at least.

Harry Potter: Harry is a powerful wizard, but when it comes to spells, transfigurations, potions, and wielding a wand, Hermione is the best of them all. She's the top student of her class.

Sideways: Miles is a natural at tasting wine, but Maya is the one with the sharpest palate. And she's studying horticulture to become a wine grower.

Dodgeball: They all are natural dodgeball players—except Justin: He is a natural male cheerleader. But Kate is faster, stronger, and more precise than anyone else.

Related:
104 – The Hero's Improvement

086 – Atonement: First Foreshadow

At the climax of the story there will be an Atonement with the Father.

Description:

This stage compares the Hero to his father by showing a trait that both share, either a positive or a negative one.

This stage presents the father's backstory, showing how he dealt with the same challenge that the Hero will have to face.

This happens in anticipation of the Hero's supreme choice: To be or not to be like the father. (Answer: None of the above—see related stages).

Examples:

Star Wars: Anakin was the strongest with the Force, but he succumbed to the Dark Side. That risk is ever present in Luke, too: Will he succumb, or will he resist?

The Matrix: Neo's fatherly figure is Morpheus, who's all about belief. But Neo will need to transcend mere belief. That's the only way he can see beyond the Prophecy.

Harry Potter: Harry's father sacrificed himself to protect his loved ones, and Harry will face the same destiny. But he will prevail where his father couldn't.

Sideways: Miles is compared to the "father" character in the novel he wrote, whose story ends badly. Will Miles's story end like that, as well?

Dodgeball: (Not applicable).

Related:

121 – Atonement: Second Foreshadow
181 – Atonement

087 – World under Surveillance

The ordinary people get restrained, scattered, imprisoned, or sent into exile.

Description:

Not every story has to be about an evil empire controlling the galaxy, but the dominion of evil must expand somehow. And things will get even worst as the story progresses.

Examples:

Star Wars: The dominion of the Empire across multiple star systems grows. "The more you tighten your grip, Tarkin, the more star systems will slip through your fingers," Leia says.

The Matrix: Morpheus explains that humanity is controlled by Machines. He paraphrases Baudrillard: "Welcome to the desert of the Real."

Harry Potter: Hagrid mentions that Voldemort is not dead but hiding somewhere. Indeed, The Dark Lord uses Quirrell to get access to Hogwarts. He's right there, watching everything.

Sideways: Miles lives with a dark companion over his shoulder: His depression, which is mentioned a few times, either directly, or indirectly by referencing his therapist, his medication, etc.

Dodgeball: A huge monitor at Globo Gym shows White Goodman controlling everyone: "You call that a sit-up? Don't slack, Trevor. I'm watching you!"

Related:

014 – The World in Decline
035 – The Villain's Dominion

088 – Good Guys in Disagreement
The good guys still don't know what needs to be done.

Description:

The opinions of the peers prevail over our Hero's; their plan is accepted despite the Hero's resistance. That plan will fail, of course.

Nuking an asteroid, sending a helicopter to communicate with the alien mothership, or shooting first and asking questions later—whatever is done, it ends up in catastrophe.

Examples:

Star Wars: Han's ship follows a solitary TIE Fighter to a small moon. Luke warns that it's not a moon, but a battle station. Han disagrees: "It is too big to be a battle station." Well, it *is* a battle station, and they just got caught in its tractor beam.

The Matrix: Cypher asks Trinity, "You like watching him, don't you?" Trinity replies, "Don't be ridiculous." Cypher says, "We're going to kill him. Do you understand that?" Cypher will indeed try to kill Neo, which will not work as he expects (see 132 – Attack 9: The Hero's Lair).

Harry Potter: Harry knows that the sorcerer's stone is at risk of being stolen. The professors dismiss his concerns. They're wrong.

Sideways: Miles proposes starting the wine tour at the other end of the valley, so the drunker they are, the closer to the hotel they are. Jack doesn't care about wine; he just wants to have sex with a woman. The two have an argument.

Dodgeball: Instead of the uniforms they ordered, the team receives a box full of sadomasochistic, erotic outfits. Kate and Dwight refuse to play using those, but they are forced by the circumstances. The public at the arena doesn't take that very well.

Related:
137 – Recrimination by Ally

089 – A Bad Feeling about This
Some character expresses pessimism.

Description:

This stage is an Omen of impending catastrophe.

Some character says something like "I smell trouble," "I have a bad feeling about this," or "this is not going to end well."

This stage can also adopt the opposite form: "Everything is going to be okay." It will not.

Examples:

Star Wars: As the Millennium Falcon is hauled to the Death Star by the tractor beam, Luke says, "I have a very bad feeling about this." C3PO says it all the time, of course.

The Matrix: Cypher warns Neo, "Fasten your seat belt, Dorothy, because Kansas is gonna bye-bye."

Harry Potter: The kids find themselves in the forbidden corridor. Harry says, "Does anyone feel like we shouldn't be here?"

Sideways: Jack insists that Miles must approach Maya. Miles answers, "She's a fucking waitress in Buellton. How would that ever work?"

Dodgeball: Dwight predicts, "We're gonna get our taints handed to us!" Jason asks, "What's a taint?" Gordon says: "I don't know. It sounds bad".

Related:
127 – A Suicide Mission

090 – Blindness Symbolism
Awakening is still a long way ahead.

Description:

The Hero is still "blind"—blind to his true potential, to the plans and power of the dark side, and to the growing attraction with the Goddess.

This is shown metaphorically by introducing some reference to ignorance, disorientation, or even literal blindness.

Examples:

Star Wars: Luke trains in the use of the lightsaber using a blinding helmet. What Luke doesn't *see* yet, though, is the power of the Force that resides in him.

The Matrix: Neo and Morpheus arrive at the Oracle's building. A blind man greets them with a nod, as if he could see Morpheus's nod. The blind one here, though, is Neo who has to see the world and himself for what they really are.

Harry Potter: Harry uses an invisibility cloak to move around, and no one can see him infiltrating the Library. The oil lamp falling and breaking is also symbolic of the lack of sight or light.

Sideways: Miles attributes Maya's kindness to the fact that she works for tips. Jack tells him, "You're blind, dude. Blind." What Miles refuses to see is the mutual attraction he and Maya have.

Dodgeball: Patches asks Peter to blindfold himself and learn to dodge balls without seeing them. What Peter has yet to see is his crucial role as leader of the team.

Related:

084 – Snake Symbolism
185 – Consummation of Love

091 – Attack 4: Interrogation

The Villain tries to extract information from the Hero.

Description:

The Hero has entered the radar of the Villain. However, the Villain hasn't yet realized the magnitude of the threat the Hero poses.

In this stage, we see the dark side's methods up close. There is an interrogation or a demand, but the Hero refuses to collaborate, even under duress.

Examples:

Star Wars: Darth Vader enters Leia's cell and demands to know the location of the Rebel base. A scary interrogation drone with a needle hovers toward the Princess. She resists the torture.

The Matrix: Neo is interrogated by the Agents. He gives them the finger. Later on, Morpheus will resist their terrible methods, too.

Harry Potter: Just before the Sorting Hat ceremony, Malfoy tries to recruit Harry for his cabal. Harry refuses.

Sideways: Jack tries to put Miles into party mood. Miles just want to go back to the motel and crash.

Dodgeball: White tries to seduce Kate. She says, "Sorry, I vomited a little bit inside my mouth."

Related:

033 – Attack 3: The Hero Resists
092 – Attack 5: Spying

092 – Attack 5: Spying
The dark side conducts some intelligence task.

Description:

The Hero refused to collaborate with the dark side, so now the Villain has to try a different method: Spying. The Villain uses tracking devices, cameras, microphones, spies, cell phones... Anything that works.

The maneuver works for a while, until the Goddess discovers and neutralizes it. Nonetheless, the Villain is able to develop a plan based on the information obtained.

Examples:

Star Wars: Once the Millennium Falcon has escaped the Death Star, Leia warns Luke and Han that the ship is surely being tracked with a beacon. Han dismisses her suspicion, but she is right, of course.

The Matrix: Smith inserts a "bug" (a disgusting insect-like tracking device) in Neo. Trinity extracts it and throws it out the car's window.

Harry Potter: Malfoy spies on Harry and turns him in, because Harry was outside after hours. Professor McGonagall puts Harry in detention, but she punishes Malfoy, too (a passage I also refer to in stage 129 - The Villain's Shadow).

Sideways: Christine calls Jack insistently, wanting to know what is he up to; Miles makes excuses for him. Note that Christine is not a Villain and Miles is a not Goddess, but the stage is there, anyway.

Dodgeball: White Goodman puts a life-sized cardboard cutout of himself inside Peter's Gym. It is meant as an insult, but it also contains a hidden camera. Kate destroys the camera by throwing a fastball to the figure's head.

Related:
091 – Attack 4: Interrogations

093 – Baptism of Fire: Failure
The Hero faces the first battle or challenge.

Description:

This stage introduces the Hero's first real test: A battle, a fight, a discussion, a dangerous situation, confrontation, a game, etc. The Hero fails, and the reason is once more the Hero's Weakness.

This stage creates doubts about the Hero, but not disappointment: The audience must keep rooting for the Hero.

Examples:

Star Wars: Luke is confronted by two criminals in the cantina. He fails to deflect their provocation. One of the criminals pulls a gun and takes aim at Luke, intending to kill him. Luke doesn't react to the aggression in time.

The Matrix: Neo jumps between the two buildings and falls all the way down to the pavement.

Harry Potter: Harry confronts a troll in the girl's bathroom. He fails to use his wand. The troll grabs him from one leg. His wand is gone, and he's about to be killed.

Sideways: In his first real talk with Maya, Miles misses an opportunity to get a date. Maya leaves.

Dodgeball: Average Joe's plays a qualifying match against Troop 417, a team of Girl Scouts. They lose miserably.

Related:
070 – Baptism of Water
094 – Baptism of Fire: Rescue

ACT 2.1 — ROAD OF TRIALS

094 – Baptism of Fire: Rescue

The Mentor (or some other ally) brings the Hero back to life.

Description:

The Hero lives to fight another day, but there is a physical wound involved in this stage. The Baptism of Fire is an instance of Transmogrification (stage 044), so we need to see some blood here.

This first resurrection is not the work of the Goddess, though. Keep her miracle in reserve for later.

Examples:

Star Wars: Just before Luke gets shot, Obi-Wan ignites his lightsaber with blinding speed and swiftly eliminates the threat. On the floor we see a cut-off arm laying in a puddle of blood.

The Matrix: Tank, who controls the training simulation, turns the pavement into a flexible surface so Neo doesn't die on impact. Neo leaves the program with blood in his mouth, though.

Harry Potter: Ron casts the levitation spell on the Troll, saving Harry. The three kids end up with scratches from the violent fight.

Sideways: Jack seduces Stephanie, who knows Maya. This gives rise to a new chance for Miles to approach Maya.

Dodgeball: Troop 417 is disqualified because one of girls tested positive for "three separate types of anabolic steroids and a beaver tranquilizer." Average Joe's qualifies. They are all hurting from the violence of the little girls' shots, though.

Related:
070 – Baptism of Water
093 – Baptism of Fire: Failure
166 – The Hero's Resurrection

095 – Attack 6: Intimidation
The Villain makes a demonstration of power.

Description:

Spying on the Hero didn't work as well as expected, so the Villain launches a new offensive. This is a psychological attack, another step in the escalating virulence of the Villain's actions.

The Hero resists but doesn't fight back.

Examples:

Star Wars: Leia resists torture. Vader tells Tarkin, "It will be some time before we can extract any information from her."

The Matrix: The Agents pin Neo down on a table and say, "You are going to help us whether you want it or not, Mr. Anderson." They insert the bug through his navel. Neo resists.

Harry Potter: Draco Malfoy shows his proficiency in flying on a broomstick; he takes Neville's remembrall and threatens to destroy it. Harry defends his friend.

Sideways: Jack rebukes Miles because he didn't approach Maya. Miles resists the attack by inventing excuses.

Dodgeball: White Goodman and his team show up at the restaurant for a vain demonstration of power. They bully the group of celebrating friends.

Related:
092 – Attack 5: Spying
102 – Attack 7: False Enemy

096 – The Hero Is Recognized

Somebody recognizes the Hero. A reference to the legend behind the Hero is made.

Description:

The Hero's arc continues evolving from anonymity to popularity. Some minor character recognizes the Hero and the Hero's accomplishments.

The stakes rise, because of the expectations deposited on the Hero have grown.

Examples:

Star Wars: Luke remains anonymous, but there is another "legend" in this story: "You've never heard of the Millennium Falcon? It's the ship that made the Kessel run in less than twelve parsecs!" says Han, trying to impress Obi-Wan.

The Matrix: Neo arrives at the Oracle's apartment. An unknown woman opens the door and tells him, "Hello, Neo. You're just in time."

Harry Potter: Everyone who crosses paths with Harry recognizes the name; for example, the patrons at the Leaky Cauldron: "Bless my soul—it's Harry Potter"; "Welcome back, Mr. Potter, welcome back"; "Doris Crockford, Mr. Potter. I can't believe I'm meeting you at last."

Sideways: Everyone congratulates Miles when Jack talks about the (non-existent) book deal.

Dodgeball: At the restaurant, Patches recognizes Peter from the match against the Girl Scouts. "That was the worst damn display of dodgeball I've seen in years," Patches says.

Related:
063 – The Hero Is Welcome

097 – Right Words at the Right Time (1)
The Hero receives a piece of wisdom.

Description:

The Right Words contain the message, or moral, of the story.

Not much happens when these words are pronounced. In fact, the scene usually ends right there. These words, however, sink deep in the Hero's consciousness.

The Right Words are not just motivational; they are an existential truth that will eventually allow the Hero to let go of the Weakness, to trust his talents, and to win this thing.

Examples:

Star Wars: These words have become part of a generation: "May the Force be with you." That conviction is what gives Luke the final victory.

The Matrix: "Do not try and bend the spoon. That's impossible," a kid dressed in Buddhist robes tells Neo. "Instead, only try to realize the truth: There is no spoon." These words eventually allow Neo to see the Matrix for what it really is: Just an illusion.

Harry Potter: In *The Deathly Hallows* Harry's parents say, "We will be with you, always," before he faces death at the hands of Voldemort.

Sideways: Maya tells Miles, "The day you open a '61 Cheval Blanc, that's the special occasion." The message is: Stop letting life slip through his fingers, leave the past behind, and live the moment.

Dodgeball: Patches gives Peter his scarf. "You're a hell of a player, Peter. You earned it," Patches says. And then he adds, "Hey, I've got some hookers in my room. What do you say we go celebrate? My treat." Peter accepts the scarf but passes on the invitation.

Related:
170 – Right Words at the Right Time (2)

098 – The Awkward Innocent

The Hero shows kindness toward someone who is usually shunned by others.

Description:

The Awkward Innocent is a kid, a rookie, or someone socially awkward who is trying to fit in. Others shun this person, but the Hero shows tolerance.

Note that the role of the Awkward Innocent is to point out candid truths, while the role of the Oblivious Innocent (stage 159) is to show cluelessness. Both can be used to comedic effect.

Examples:

Star Wars: C3PO makes irrelevant observations all the time. Luke listens to him, but Han shuns the droid: "Never tell me the odds!"

The Matrix: Mouse bothers Neo with philosophical conundrums. Neo listens patiently. The others make Mouse shut up.

Harry Potter: There are several characters like this: Dobby the Elf, Colin Creevey, Grawp the Giant, and especially Luna Lovegood.

Sideways: Jack does taste the strawberry in his pinot, but that's because he is chewing gum. Miles reprimands him but also shows him patience.

Dodgeball: "I'm just saying, it happens," Dwight says, justifying his prediction about Jason's rival falling from a roller coaster. "My cousin Ray-Ray? Boop. Dead."

Related:
159 – The Oblivious Innocent

ROAD OF TRIALS — The Ultimate Hero's Journey — ACT **2.1**

099 – The Lieutenant's Ineptitude

If you want something done, take the matter in your own hands.

Description:

The good guys are getting better, to the point that they outplay a major dark side lieutenant. The Villain gets angry and decides to personally take care of the task.

Examples:

Star Wars: The Millennium Falcon escapes from the Death Star. Darth Vader mind-chokes and kills a captain responsible for the failure. In the final battle, Vader takes matters in his own hands by piloting a fighter against the Rebels.

The Matrix: The police lieutenant says, "We can handle one little girl", in reference to Trinity. Agent Smith answers, "No, Lieutenant, your men are already dead," and heads inside the abandoned hotel to finish the job himself.

Harry Potter: Quirrell is unable to extract the truth from Harry, so Voldemort, despite being still weak, decides to face Harry personally.

Sideways: Miles would never take the initiative in approaching the two women, so Jack has to take the lead.

Dodgeball: The girl can indeed throw a ball. White says, "I'll simply have to woo Kate a bit sooner than nature intended," and tries to seduce her. He ends up getting crushed against a wall, and he deserved it.

100 – Presentation of Gifts
The Hero receives a gift from the Goddess.

Description:

The Goddess, who incarnates a life-giving force, gives the Hero something that helps to succeed in the next trials. This artifact will be of critical importance during the attacks that follow, all of which lead to the Final Battle.

Examples:

Star Wars: Luke officially receives Leia's droids. C3PO tells R2D2, "It's all right, you can trust him. He's our new master."

The Matrix: Neo receives a cookie from the Oracle. It makes Neo feel better and prepares him for a defining decision: Either to save himself or to save Morpheus.

Harry Potter: Harry receives Christmas gifts from Mrs. Weasley (Ron's mother, in a Goddess role) and a brand new flying broomstick from Professor McGonagall.

Sideways: Miles receives two boxes of wine from Stephanie's winery. Jack paid for them, though.

Dodgeball: Like Neo, Peter receives homemade cookies: Kate was baking some.

Related:
045 – The Herald's Gift

ROAD OF TRIALS — The Ultimate Hero's Journey — ACT **2.1**

101 – The Temptress
The Hero is tempted to stray from the path.

Description:

The Hero faces yet another test: A temptress with a seductive offer. If obstacles don't work, maybe detours will.

The Temptress isn't always a woman; it can also be feminine energy or some entity representing good emotions and sensuality. This character or artifact is not directly related to the dark side, but it represents the (erotic, material, etc.) temptations of the Ordinary World.

The Hero either ignores the temptation or negotiates a compromise.

Examples:

Star Wars: Two beautiful girls, the Tonnika sisters, stare with curiosity at Luke when he enters the Cantina. He ignores them and walks away, following Obi-Wan.

The Matrix: Dujour, the girl with the White Rabbit tattoo, tempts Neo into going to a party with her and her friends. Neo accepts because of Trinity's message ("Follow the White Rabbit").

Harry Potter: Temptation for kids has a name: Sweets. The Cart Lady offers to sell sweets to the kids, but Ron rejects the offer: He holds in his hand a disgusting sandwich his mother prepared. Harry buys the lot, though.

Sideways: Stephanie teases Jack by serving full cups of an expensive Estate Syrah. Jack tells her she's a bad girl. She answers, "Yes, and I need to be spanked." Jack negotiates a date with her and Maya.

Dodgeball: Peter is the tempter. He tries to convince Kate to join the team using a bribing package. She accepts, but for different reasons. Those movie passes were expired, anyway.

Related:
152 – Temptation Rejected

102 – Attack 7: False Enemy

The audience is lead to suspect the wrong character.

Description:

The False Enemy makes a move against the Hero or plots to do so.

This attack is only apparent; the Hero is not being betrayed, but actually being protected.

The misdirection about this character (i.e., keeping his allegiance to light side a secret) is created by subtracting context from his actions.

Examples:

Star Wars: Chewbacca is a Wookiee, a monstrous creature that pulls people's arms out of their sockets when it loses at holographic chess—or so Han Solo says.

The Matrix: In *The Matrix Reloaded* (2003), Seraph attacks Neo. Is Seraph a real enemy? No, he did it to confirm that Neo is The One in order to grant him access to the Oracle.

Harry Potter: Harry's False Enemy is already a classic: Professor Snape, who seems to be cursing Harry's broomstick when he is actually protecting Harry from Quirrell's curse. Snape continues with his act until the end of the saga, when he sacrifices himself to protect Harry.

Sideways: In tone with the human depth of the movie, Jack is Miles's False Enemy. Jack pressures Miles to act as his wingman and seduce the girls. Despite the sexual scope of Jack intentions, the encounter with Maya ends up being the way in which Miles finds true love.

Dodgeball: (Not applicable).

Related:
095 – Attack 6: Intimidation
113 – Attack 8: Shock and Awe

103 – Maternal Love
Some character shows affection or compassion for the Hero.

Description:

A motherly figure shows love for the Hero despite the Hero's Immaturity and Weakness.

She loves the Hero not for being the One (as the Mentor does), nor in a romantic way (as the romantic interest character does), nor because the Hero is a savior (as other people do), but simply because of the person the Hero is.

Examples:

Star Wars: Aunt Beru is the closest to a mother that Luke has. She worries and advocates for him. "Luke's just not a farmer, Owen. He has too much of his father in him."

The Matrix: The Oracle is the closest to a mother that Neo has. The scene in the kitchen is a show of that affection: She treats Neo kindly, offers him a cookie, and offers him consolation after he concludes that he is not The One.

Harry Potter: Professor McGonagall is the closest to a mother that Harry has. She secretly gives Harry a Nimbus 2000, the fastest model of flying broomsticks.

Sideways: Miles's mother prepares the guys an opulent dinner, offers Miles money, and throws exaggerated compliments at Jack: "That they didn't make you the biggest movie star in the world is a sin!"

Dodgeball: (Not applicable).

104 – The Hero's Improvement
Hey, the kid packs a nice punch after all.

Description:

The Hero finally surprises everyone by scoring a clear win.

The Hero's talent is in ascent (not the overall arc, which is always in descent). He or she is getting better, and people notice.

Examples:

Star Wars: Luke plan of rescuing Leia and making their way toward the Millennium Falcon succeeds.

The Matrix: Neo defeats Morpheus in his first dojo session. Mouse says, "Take a look at his neuro-kinetics. They're way above normal!"

Harry Potter: Harry gets appointed as Gryffindor's seeker—the first time ever for a first-year at Hogwarts.

Sideways: Miles is enchanting with words. "Half my life is over, and I have nothing to show for it. I'm a thumbprint on the window of a skyscraper." (Yeah, that's Bukowski. Oh, well).

Dodgeball: Average Joe's defeats Blitzkrieg, Germany's national dodgeball team. Their coach, David Hasselhoff, is not happy: "*Ihr seid alle Schweine*! Losers!"

Related:
085 – Surpassing Peers

105 – The Villain's Disturbance

The Villain is disturbed by some powerful presence.

Description:

The Villain feels the presence of either the Hero, the Mentor, or the Goddess.

The Villain is totally focused on acquiring the Boon, to the point of obsession, so this feeling has a negative psychological effect on the Villain.

Examples:

Star Wars: Vader is disturbed by the feeling of Obi-Wan's presence in the Death Star.

The Matrix: Smith tells Morpheus that he doesn't tolerate the presence of humans: "It's the smell. It's repulsive, isn't it?"

Harry Potter: Just as Harry's scar hurts when Voldemort is close by, every time Quirrell encounters Harry, the professor avoids all physical contact.

Sideways: Victoria is disturbed by Miles's late call, a chat that doesn't end well.

Dodgeball: White is furious with Kate (who is working for him) because she keeps hanging out with Peter and the rest of the team at the rival gym.

Related:
009 – Mutual Creation
160 – A Cross of Swords

106 – A Well-Complemented Team
The Hero's allies have their own bag of tricks.

Description:

The team's talents are both complementary to those of the Hero (think the Watsons to your Sherlock) and also complementary to each other.

The Mentor is wise; the Goddess is talented and a natural leader. There is sometimes a big, strong character; there can be a nerd; there is a loyal sidekick; there is a mysterious character whose talent is revealed toward the end, and so on.

Examples:

Star Wars: Obi-Wan is wise, and Han is street-wise. Leia is a natural leader. Chewbacca is big and strong. C3PO is a nerd, and R2D2 is loyal.

The Matrix: Morpheus is wise, Trinity is a natural leader, Dozer is big and strong, Tank is a nerd, and Mouse is loyal.

Harry Potter: Dumbledore is wise, Hermione is a natural leader and a nerd, Hagrid is big and strong, and Ron is loyal.

Sideways: These characters are fused in a more realistic, non-archetypal way. Also, the talents in romantic stories are different from those in an epic story or from those in a thriller, or other genres.

Dodgeball: Patches is street-wise but also a homophobic bigot. Gordon is a nerd but also a wimp. Jason is loyal but kind of a loser. They all have their own weaknesses to overcome, it seems. Kate is the most normal person in the team, and a natural leader.

Related Stage:
108 – People Take Sides

107 – Breaking the Law
In fiction, rules exist to one end: To get broken.

Description:

Going by the book won't work. Extraordinary achievements demand extraordinary tactics.

The Hero does the opposite of what the rules order, and does it with little remorse—a result of the Hero's disregard for authority.

Examples:

Star Wars: In a galaxy dominated by a fascist Empire, everything Luke and friends do goes against the rules.

The Matrix: For Neo, breaking the rules of the world and breaking through his own limitations are one and the same thing. Morpheus tells him, "What are you waiting for? You're faster than this."

Harry Potter: Where do the three kids go during the night? They go to the forbidden third floor corridor, to the Forbidden Forest, to a cave full of giant spiders, and every other place they were expressly told to avoid.

Sideways: The guys pour wine in their cups when the server is not looking, they fake a car accident, and they lie about a few other things, too.

Dodgeball: This story goes the other way, once again: What saves the team is precisely rules--the Dodgeball Rule Book that Gordon always carries with him.

Related:
075 – Book of Laws

108 – People Take Sides

Allegiances around both the Hero and the Villain become clearer.

Description:

We see both teams holding separate meetings, as a symbol of the consolidation of the theme.

The Hero is the underdog and appeals to castaways, rebels, uncomprehended geniuses, truly noble people, and some shady character who adds a dark touch to the team.

Other kinds of people coalesce around the Villain: The establishment, the fearful, the conformists, the greedy. They are all used as it better fits the Villain's ends.

Examples:

Star Wars: In *The Revenge of the Sith* (2005), Darth Sidious holo-meets his lackeys: The members of the Federation of Commerce, fearful senators, and separatist planet leaders. On the other hand, the Rebel Alliance is formed by ex-Jedi, smugglers, lost droids, and freedom fighters.

The Matrix: We see the three Agents working together in the Matrix, and Morpheus's crew working together in the real world.

Harry Potter: The Quidditch game is a symbol of polarity: The brave Gryffindors versus the cunning and brutal Slytherins.

Sideways: Jack and Miles represent the good guys' team and the bad guys' team at the same time. The struggle is internal.

Dodgeball: Here the teams are literal: Average Joe's and the Purple Cobras both defeat their opponents, which puts them on a collision course with each other.

Related Stage:

106 – A Well-Complemented Team

109 – Praise to the Great Mentor

Some characters praises the Mentor, thankful of having him on their side.

Description:

As long as the good guys have the Mentor on their side, they have a chance. The problem is: That situation is not going to last for long.

This stage is a foreshadowing one: The Mentor is praised in anticipation to the character's fall. The word "great" is usually in order.

Examples:

Star Wars: Obi-Wan disables the tractor beam to clear the way for escape. Han doesn't have much faith in the old man, but Luke defends his master, calling him "a great man."

The Matrix: Neo's Mentor is referred to as "the great Morpheus." The Oracle says, "Without him we are lost."

Harry Potter: Dumbledore is referred to as "the greatest headmaster Hogwarts has ever seen." Hermione tells Harry, "As long as Dumbledore's around, you're safe."

Sideways: Jack proposes a toast: "It's going to be great. Here's to us."

Dodgeball: Average Joe's wins another match. "As long as we got Patches, we got a shot," says Peter. The ESPN-8 commentator says, "With Patches O'Houlihan at the helm, I guess it must be the luck of the Irish."

Related:
114 – The Mentor's Orders
116 – The Mentor Is Gone

110 – Run for Your Life (1)
The current strategy: Survive.

Description:

The Hero and friends are still trying to figure out what the hell is going on. In the meantime, they make decisions on the spot. Tactical decisions. Okay: They run.

You know who has a plan, though? That's right—the Villain. The plan has only one weakness: It underestimates the Hero.

Examples:

Star Wars: Luke, Han, and Leia just want to escape the Death Star. The Empire is focused on finding the location of the Rebel base. Darth Vader sensed Obi-Wan's presence but failed to sense Luke's.

The Matrix: The good guys' only strategy right now is to escape from the Matrix before they get caught. The Agents are focused on capturing Morpheus. They didn't kill Neo when they could have. "They have underestimated how important you are," Morpheus says.

Harry Potter: Quirrell is focused on acquiring the sorcerer's stone; Harry only tries not to get killed by his cursed broomstick.

Sideways: Jack is focused on seducing Stephanie; Miles's plan is to go back to the hotel and sleep.

Dodgeball: Peter La Fleur with a plan? Are you kidding me? He hasn't even returned *Backdoor Patrol 5* and *Mona Lisa Smile* to the video store!

Related:
123 – Run for Your Life (2)
158 – Run for Your Life (3)

111 – Traitor on the Move
Judas seals the deal.

Description:

Most stories have their Judas: Double agents, spies, or traitors. That's not counting self-sabotage: We can be our own worst enemies sometimes.

The identity of the Traitor is revealed here, and we get to understand this character's motivation, too. Is it revenge? Money? Power? Whatever it is, it's personal and hateful.

Examples:

Star Wars: The closest to a traitor or a liar is Governor Tarkin. He promises Leia he won't destroy Alderaan if she reveals the location of the Rebel base, but as soon as he gets an answer, he orders to fire all the same. Tarkin's objective is to terrorize the galaxy into submission.

The Matrix: Cypher is eating a steak at a fine restaurant in the Matrix, sealing the deal with Agent Smith. Cypher's motivation: Bitter revenge from Morpheus, and getting a way out of the Real World, which he can't stand anymore.

Harry Potter: Quirrell's body hosts Voldemort's spirit. Harry meets the evil figure in a clearing in the Dark Forest.

Sideways: At the restaurant, Miles promised not to drink too much and not go to the dark side, but he does exactly that: He couldn't get over the news of his ex-wife remarrying.

Dodgeball: This stage happens later on, when Peter himself succumbs to White's bribe (another instance of self-sabotage).

Related:
074 – The Traitor

112 – The Villain's True Face
Now we see what the Hero is up against. And it's terrifying.

Description:

We have seen the Villain talking, scheming, and chasing. But we haven't seen the Villain acting. Well, this is when his patience reaches the end of the road.

Scare your audience. Make them believe that defeating this magnificent evil is impossible.

Examples:

Star Wars: That moon-sized, planet-destroying war machine is certainly scary, but we haven't seen what it is capable of. Now Tarkin gives the order to initiate the firing sequence.

The Matrix: The Agents, who until now looked like humans, are revealed to be something else. Somehow they can teleport in or out of other people, they never run of ammo, and they never die.

Harry Potter: We have heard of Voldemort and the fear that his name inspires; they refer to him as the most powerful dark wizard in history. But we are about to see him for what he is these days: A murderous, evil, perverted form of life.

Sideways: Jack is getting laid before his wedding, and nobody will stop him. It's going to happen. Tonight. He distributes condoms: One for Miles, three for himself.

Dodgeball: What can be more irresistible than White Goodman in his shiny shoes? "I'm here to begin my courtship of you, Kate." The rest of his speech would be pathetic if it weren't so crazy.

Related:

035 – The Villain's Dominion
125 – The Über-Villain
149 – The Villain's Grand Entrance

113 – Attack 8: Shock and Awe
The Villain takes his most aggressive step yet.

Description:

This attack hits hard—very hard. It is a token of the ultimate catastrophe that will occur if the Villain is allowed to succeed all the way.

This attack is not directed against the Hero but subservient to the Villain's goals. Also, this attack usually starts a chain of events that ends up causing the Mentor's fall.

Examples:

Star Wars: The Death Star shoots Alderaan, Leia's home, obliterating it. Obi-Wan is overwhelmed by the disturbance this event caused in The Force.

The Matrix: Cypher takes a huge ray gun and attacks The Nebuchadnezzar's crew. Apoc, Switch, Mouse, and Dozer are killed, Tank is left for dead, and Morpheus is taken prisoner.

Harry Potter: Voldemort kills a unicorn to drink its blood. (I had to fast-forward the movie during that part).

Sideways: Jack finally gets what he wanted. He makes noisy love with Stephanie.

Dodgeball: Average Joe's is decimated by the Poughkeepsie State Flying Cougars. Only Gordon remains; everyone else is eliminated.

Related:
102 – Attack 7: False Enemy
132 – Attack 9: The Hero's Lair

114 – The Mentor's Orders
Last instructions before going into battle.

Description:

The Mentor was never meant to face the ultimate challenge himself. This role is one of guidance, wisdom, and ultimately, sacrifice. At some point in the story the Mentor is killed or neutralized, and this stage marks the beginning of the end for the Mentor.

Examples:

Star Wars: Obi-Wan orders Luke to leave: "Your destiny lies along a different path than mine."

The Matrix: Morpheus orders Trinity, "You must get Neo out. He's all that matters."

Harry Potter: Firenze the Centaur (stepping into a Mentor role) protects Harry from the hooded figure and tells him to leave the Dark Forest.

Sideways: (Not applicable).

Dodgeball: Patches calls time out, just when Gordon is about to get creamed and the match lost.

Related:
036 – The Villain's Orders
115 – The Mentor's Fight
116 – The Mentor Is Gone

115 – The Mentor's Fight
The Mentor faces the forces of evil.

Description:

The Mentor confronts the Villain personally and looses the fight, of course—the only one who could defeat the Villain is the Hero. Possibly.

But this is what the Villain ignores: This fight was anticipated, and even intended by the Mentor. It's part of the Mentor's plan.

Examples:

Star Wars: Obi-Wan comes out of his hiding place and crosses Vader. They meet in a duel of lightsabers.

The Matrix: Morpheus comes out of his hiding place and confronts the police assault team. He fights bravely, outgunned and outnumbered.

Harry Potter: Dumbledore's moment comes in *The Half-Blood Prince*; Snape kills him, which puts in motion the last part of his complex (and genius) plan to defeat Voldemort. We don't learn until the following movie that Snape did it because Dumbledore ordered him to.

Sideways: Some golfers shoot a ball at the guys. Jack chases the bullies away, screaming obscenities and wielding a golf club like it was a medieval mace.

Dodgeball: Patches tells Gordon to get angry; it's the only chance to save the game.

Related:
114 – The Mentor's Orders
116 – The Mentor Is Gone

116 – The Mentor Is Gone

The Mentor dies, is taken prisoner, or becomes unavailable.

Description:

The Mentor's sacrifice has two purposes: 1) to protect the Hero until the Hero is totally ready, and 2) to weaken the Villain in anticipation of the final battle.

The Mentor will return, though, even if only as a memory in the Hero's mind.

Examples:

Star Wars: Obi-Wan is stricken down by Darth Vader. Obi-Wan sacrifices himself to save Luke (some say Obi-Wan transfers his Force to Luke, some say he becomes a Force spirit when he dies, which is the reason why his body simply vanishes). Luke escapes.

The Matrix: Morpheus is beaten down and taken prisoner. He sacrifices himself to save Neo, who is able to escape.

Harry Potter 6: Dumbledore allows Draco to disarm him, so the loyalty of the Alder Wand is never transferred to Snape or Voldemort. Then Dumbledore offers his ultimate sacrifice: He begs Snape to kill him. The Slytherin master follows the terrible mandate; it is the only to win Voldemort's trust.

Sideways: Jack is gone; he leaves Miles alone and spends time with Stephanie and her family.

Dodgeball: Patches O'Houlihan gets crushed by a two-ton electric sign that reads "The Luck of the Irish."

Related:
114 – The Mentor's Orders
115 – The Mentor's Fight

117 – A Moment of Reflection
The Hero stops the ball and thinks. Finally.

Description:

The Hero realizes that nothing is working and that running forever isn't an option.

The Hero has to come up with a game-changing plan and have one, yet. But a light bulb is about to shine in the Hero's head.

Examples:

Star Wars: Luke and Han have locked themselves in the control room of the detention block. Luke thinks for a second and comes up with a new plan.

The Matrix: The only way to prevent the Agents from obtaining the codes is unplugging Morpheus. Just when Tank is about to do it, Neo thinks for second and says, "Stop."

Harry Potter: Christmas break. Harry is frustrated because he couldn't find anything about Flamel in the library. Then he receives a hint from Hermione.

Sideways: Miles and Maya go to the porch and sit in silence for a second. There's no plan per se; they just wanted to leave the house because of the noisy lovemaking happening back there.

Dodgeball: Peter leaves the group and heads to his room. Patches's death took a high toll on him.

Related:
120 – Plan B: Rescue

118 – The Ultimate Boon
Some detail gives up what the Villain's main plan is.

Description:

After the last attack (stage 113 – Attack 8: Shock and Awe) a little Christmas gift was left in the rubble: A small clue of some kind. That detail, combined with a piece of information provided by the Goddess, allows the Hero to understand what the Villain's ultimate objective is.

Examples:

Star Wars: The Empire's Ultimate Boon is to find the location of the Rebel base to blow it out of the sky, of course. But suddenly, R2D2 begins to whistle; C3PO translates: "He says 'I found her,' and keeps repeating, 'She's here.'"

The Matrix: The Ultimate Boon is Morpheus. He knows the Zion's mainframe access codes. Neo learns this from Tank and Trinity.

Harry Potter: Voldemort's Ultimate Boon is the sorcerer's stone. That way he can get back to life (see next stage, 119).

Sideways: Miles and Maya discover love in each other through their love for wine. This realization happens in the central dialogue of the movie (see next stage, 119).

Dodgeball: The little detail is that, out of the corner of his eye, Gordon sees his mail-order wife flirting with David Hasselhoff. Rage takes Gordon over, which is precisely the key to win the match. The Ultimate Boon is the dodgeball championship and the $50,000, of course.

Related:
119 – Second Epiphany

119 – Second Epiphany

The Revelation about the Ultimate Boon gives the Hero an idea.

Description:

Knowing what the villain's Boon is, inspires the Hero to come up with a new plan (which is not disclosed to the audience, yet).

The Hero's plan—don't tell anyone—is not about attacking the Villain, but about obtaining some specific, valuable resource (see 120 – Plan B: Rescue).

This is the midpoint of your story. After this stage, the good guys stop merely reacting to the circumstances and start implementing some plans—plans that don't always work.

Examples:

Star Wars: Luke understands what R2D2 is talking about: Leia is kept prisoner right there in the Death Star, and she is scheduled for execution.

The Matrix: Neo realizes that the Oracle was right: He has a choice in front of him. And he knows what he has to do next.

Harry Potter: Hermione tells Harry that he couldn't find anything about Nicholas Flamel in the library for a simple reason: He hasn't looked in the Restricted Section. Harry develops a new plan.

Sideways: Maya discovers Miles's true personality. Miles talks about pinot, but she realizes that he is unconsciously talking about himself. This scene has the best acting of the movie.

Dodgeball: Gordon realizes that his rage is the key to victory. He gets furious and mercilessly eliminates the opponents, one by one.

Related Stage:

061 – First Epiphany
120 – Plan B: Rescue
142 – Third Epiphany

120 – Plan B: Rescue

The Hero has a new plan. No, I can't tell you about it.

Description:

The insights provided by the Second Epiphany drive the Hero into action with renovated impulse. The Hero has a plan, but we don't know what it's about.

Examples:

Star Wars: Luke and Han rescue Leia, a move the Empire didn't expect.

The Matrix: Neo and Trinity march to rescue Morpheus, a move the Agents didn't expect.

Harry Potter: Harry and Ron march to rescue Hermione from the Troll, a move that nobody expects. In the last two parts of the series, they go hunting horcruxes.

Sideways: Maya explains why she's into wine, taking Miles by the hand. An emotive rescue, both subtle and memorable.

Dodgeball: Gordon rescues the team from sure defeat, an accomplishment that nobody expected.

Related:

064 – Plan A: Let Events Unfold
143 – Plan C: Infiltrate

121 – Atonement: Second Foreshadow

The Hero faces a cursed choice.

Description:

The Hero usually has two fatherly figures who are examples of what the Hero could become. None of those options are good enough.

The Hero has a third option, though: Not repeating the path of the fatherly figures, but walking his own.

Examples:

Star Wars: Luke can either become a Jedi like Obi-Wan or a Sith like Vader. But he has another option: To succeed where both Obi-Wan (as a Jedi master) and Anakin (as a Jedi) failed.

The Matrix: Neo has two fatherly figures: Morpheus (human) and the Architect (Machine). Through exercising *choice*, Neo will eventually succeed where Morpheus, the Architect, and all the previous "Ones" have failed.

Harry Potter: Harry won't hesitate a second to become like his father or like Dumbledore. But he will eventually prevail where they couldn't.

Sideways: Miles's fatherly figure is the "father" character of his novel, who is supposedly based in Miles actual father. Miles has the chance of transcending both the real and the fictitious father.

Dodgeball: Peter's only fatherly figure is Patches O'Houlihan. And Peter has the chance to surpass Patches's glory in the world of Dodgeball, but more importantly, he has the chance of surpassing himself.

Related:

086 – Atonement: First Foreshadow
181 – Atonement

122 – The Hero Leads

The Hero is not only a weapon but also a leader.

Description:

The Hero begins to show a leadership role. The team follows, even when there are doubts about the Hero's proficiency as the new boss.

Examples:

Star Wars: Luke takes the lead. He persuades Han to rescue the Princess by telling him, "She's rich. If you were to rescue her, the reward would be more wealth that you can imagine."

The Matrix: Trinity is the highest ranking officer aboard the ship, but Neo is the one calling the shots now.

Harry Potter: Harry is a natural leader. At eleven, he makes his own decisions despite what professors, enemies, and even friends might say.

Sideways: Miles gets (amicably) pushed around by Jack's outgoing personality, but at the end, when Jack crumbles, Miles takes charge of the situation.

Dodgeball: This example again takes the opposite approach. Peter was always the natural leader of the team, but he can't stand it anymore.

Related:

148 – Rallying the Troops

123 – Run for Your Life (2)

The shocked Hero wants to stay and fight, but must escape.

Description:

The Hero has to run again for dear life. This is not cowardly fleeing from the battle but a necessary tactic to survive and regroup. The Villain is simply too powerful.

Examples:

Star Wars: Luke hears Obi-Wan's voice: "Run, Luke! Run!"

The Matrix: Neo cannot get out of the Matrix. Trinity says, "Run, Neo! Run!"

Harry Potter: Fluffy, the giant three-headed dog guarding the sorcerer's stone is awake. Harry tells his friends: "Jump! Go!"

Sideways: Jack seduced Cammi, a waiter he met in some restaurant. They were making love when her husband arrived home earlier than expected. Of course he had to run away—stark naked.

Dodgeball: Peter cannot stand the pressure of the group and runs away.

Bonus Example:

The Lord of The Rings: Gandalf is about to fall into the abyss of Moria. He tells the others, "Fly, you fools!"

Related:

110 – Run for Your Life (1)
158 – Run for Your Life (3)

124 – First Declaration of Love
The Hero and the romantic interest have a first bond.

Description:

This scene starts with romantic potential, but the circumstances impede any progress.

The obstacle can be something random, like an interruption, as usually happens in romantic movies. In other genres, the obstacle is created by the action developing around the characters.

Examples:

Star Wars: The attraction between Han and Leia is evident, but they cannot get past their strong and individualistic characters. And right now they are too busy staying alive, of course.

The Matrix: Neo asks Trinity about what the Oracle told her (that she would fall in love with The One), but she cannot answer.

Harry Potter: Kids' love. Ron mockingly imitates Hermione: "It's Levi-OH-sa, not levio-saah." Hermione hears him and hides in the bathroom to cry.

Sideways: Miles's "plan" is to go kiss Maya in Stephanie's kitchen, but the moment is long gone.

Dodgeball: Peter asks Kate, "What kind of law are you involved in, pretty eyes?" She answers, "Sexual harassment, mostly."

Related:
168 – Second Declaration of Love
185 – Consummation of Love

125 – The Über-Villain

The Villain answers to another, more powerful Villain hidden in the shadows.

Description:

The Über-Villain is a dark mentor—the Villain's boss.

This character allows room for the Villain to grow, enriching the Villain's arc. This is useful in the case of a series of novels or movies, because it adds complexity to the structure of characters and to the plot.

The Villain will eventually supersede the Über-Villain, seizing that role (or, more rarely, finding redemption, like Vader at the end of *Star Wars: Episode VI - The Return of the Jedi*.)

Examples:

Star Wars: Darth Vader answers, for now, to Emperor Palpatine, his Sith Master.

The Matrix: Agent Smith answers, for now, to the Architect, the intelligence behind the Matrix.

Harry Potter: Professor Quirrell answers to Voldemort, of course.

Sideways: Jack and Miles answer, for now, to their own whims and weaknesses.

Dodgeball: White Goodman is a slave to his own deranged narcissism.

126 – The Villain's Stronghold
We learn about the dark side's innermost cave.

Description:

The Villain's Stronghold is either the place where the Ultimate Boon is located or the place where the Hero can prevent the Villain from getting it. It is the scenario of the final battle.

The path that leads to the Villain's Stronghold is full of difficulties: Guardians, obstacles, distance, and enemies. It's like the road to Mordor, in *The Lord of the Rings*.

In this stage, however, we only get a *description* of that place; the Hero hasn't even started that road. In fact, the Hero doesn't have any idea how to get in there, and everybody else believes the Hero is crazy just for thinking about it.

Examples:

Star Wars: The Death Star has a weak spot: A small exhaust port connected to its reactor; a torpedo precisely fired through it could start a chain reaction. A pilot says, "That's impossible, even for a computer."

The Matrix: The crew finds out where Morpheus is being kept prisoner. Tank says, "Neo, this is *loco*. They've got Morpheus in a military controlled building."

Harry Potter: The kids find out where the sorcerer's stone is: Deep inside Hogwarts, behind all sorts of magical deterrents.

Sideways: Miles finds out where Jack's wedding rings are: In Cammi's room. Jack left his wallet in there, when he escaped.

Dodgeball: "Welcome to Las Vegas, a city where you can get a happy ending, but only if you pay a little extra!"

Related:
127 – A Suicide Mission
140 – The Villain's Weakness

127 – A Suicide Mission
Only a crazy person would try to get in there.

Description:

Arriving at the Stronghold is difficult, but trying to enter is just suicidal.

A plan is developed. Now, if the plan is explained to the audience, you know that it's not going to work. Only secret plans work.

Note that nobody is entering anywhere, yet. The Hero and friends are just assessing the difficulties of the mission at this point.

Everyone thinks it is a suicide mission, but the Hero sees no other option.

Examples:

Star Wars: Han says, "Attacking that battle station ain't my idea of courage. It's more like suicide."

The Matrix: Tank says, "I want Morpheus back too, but what you're talking about is suicide."

Harry Potter: Hermione says she is going to bed before Harry and Ron come up with another clever idea to get them killed, "or worse—expelled!"

Sideways: Jack's "plan" is to go back and ask for the rings. That's like asking to be killed.

Dodgeball: Average Joe's must face the Purple Cobras in the finals without Patches. Dwight says, "We'll get killed out there, Peter."

Related:
089 – A Bad Feeling about This
126 – The Villain's Stronghold

128 – The Villain's Speech

The Villain delivers a speech. Lies, lies, lies.

Description:

The Villain gains support by delivering a convincing speech, one full of promises and visions of a better future.

The Villain says it's "for justice," "for the safety of our nation," "for peace," or something else along those lines. Make the Villain sound reasonable and look like someone you would follow if you didn't know the malignant intentions behind the speech, of course.

Examples:

In **Star Wars**: In *Episode III - The Revenge of the Sith*, Palpatine gives a speech in the Galactic Senate: "In order to ensure its continuing stability, the Republic will be reorganized into the First Galactic Empire, for a safe and secure society." Everyone applauds.

The Matrix: Smith praises the Matrix: "Have you ever stood and stared at it, marveled at it's beauty, it's genius?" Then he explains to Morpheus that humans aren't mammals but viruses and that the Machines are "the cure."

Harry Potter: In *The Deathly Hallows*, Voldemort praises Pius Thicknesse, the new Minister of Magic: "Ha! Spoken like a true politician. You will, I think, prove most useful, Pius."

Sideways: Jack wants to put the wedding on hold. "I'm thinking about Christine's feelings too. I take marriage very seriously," he says.

Dodgeball: White bribes Peter: "Do you really think it's fair for them to put all that pressure on you? All the time? Looking to you to solve their every problem?"

Related:

036 – The Villain's Orders
151 – Villain's Final Allegation

129 – The Villain's Shadow

The Villain accuses the Hero of being exactly what the Villain is.

Description:

The Villain insults the Hero (or the Mentor), which paradoxically is a reflection of the Villain's own true nature.

This stage presents the archetype of the Shadow: Whatever we accuse others of, *that's* what we unconsciously are ourselves. We have to surpass ourselves, and the only way to do it is by throwing some light onto that dark part of our souls.

Sometimes Villains go a step further and exalt their own personality, as if *they* were the noble ones here. Yeah, sure.

Examples:

Star Wars: Darth Vader tells Obi-Wan, "When I left you, I was but the learner; now I am the master." Actually, Obi-Wan is still the master; Vader has a lot to learn (for example, that Luke is his son—not to mention Leia).

The Matrix: Smith tells Morpheus, "Human beings are a disease, a cancer of this planet. You are a plague." Actually, the world is plagued by Machines, and humans are just their energy source.

Harry Potter: Malfoy tells on Harry, Ron, and Hermione, accusing them of being out of the castle at night. But Malfoy was out too; that's how he got to spy on them.

Sideways: Jack recriminates Miles, ("You dumb fuck") because Miles got drunk and called his ex-wife. Actually, the "dumb fuck" in this story is Jack himself, risking everything for a sexual adventure.

Dodgeball: White tells Peter, "You are heading for a fall, Peter." But it is actually White himself who's heading that way.

Related:
105 – The Villain's Disturbance

130 – Resentment of the Mentor
The old guy left some things out.

Description:

It is revealed that the Mentor kept a part of the truth hidden.

The Hero and audience don't resent the Mentor much, though: Had the Mentor fully disclosed things, the Hero would have refused the challenge (see stage 048 – Historic Battle).

All things considered, the Mentor wasn't asking the Hero for anything the Mentor wasn't ready to give, too.

Examples:

Star Wars: In *Episode V - The Empire Strikes Back*, Luke learns that Vader is his father; Obi-Wan told him something different, of course. Luke cries desperately, his hand cut off, hanging above an abyss.

The Matrix: Cypher is enraged. "He lied to us, Trinity!" he screams, talking about Morpheus. "He tricked us!"

Harry Potter: Dumbledore took Harry as a student but never explained a tiny part of the deal: Someday, he will have to face Voldemort in a fight to death. You can't tell that to an eleven-year-old kid.

Sideways: Miles finally understands that Jack was never interested in golf or wine—only sex.

Dodgeball: Patches never said that dodgeball training involved brutal, life-threatening exercises, like dodging wrenches. Or speeding cars. Or wrenches.

ORDEAL — The Ultimate Hero's Journey — ACT **2.3**

131 – The Price of Victory
The Hero realizes that sacrifice is the only way.

Description:

This is an existential moment. Even comedies get serious here.

The Hero understands and accepts the role in the bigger scheme of things. Defeating the Villain means that the Hero will die—sometimes literally, but at least symbolically. Indeed, true sacrifice means to fight for the loved ones' happiness at the price of one's own.

Note that this is only the moment of realizing and accepting the sacrifice—not yet the moment of sacrifice itself.

Examples:

Star Wars: In *Episode VI - The Return of the Jedi*, there is a two-way realization: Luke realizes that he has to sacrifice himself to redeem Anakin; later on, Vader will realize that he has to die in order to save his son from Palpatine's fury.

The Matrix: In *Revolutions*, Neo realizes that he will have to surrender to the Machines in order to stop Smith and save humanity.

Harry Potter: Harry realizes that he will have to die in order to kill Voldemort and save humanity.

Sideways: Miles realizes that he has to "die" to his depressed, frustrated older self.

Dodgeball: Peter realizes that he has to "die" to his lazy, indolent older self in order to save his gym and his friends.

Related:
009 – Mutual Creation

132 – Attack 9: The Hero's Lair
The Villain launches another powerful attack.

Description:

The Villain doesn't want to play with his food—he wants to kill it.

The Hero's lair (home, vehicle, room, cave, or hiding place) gets destroyed, ransacked or damaged.

Examples:

Star Wars: Swarms of TIE Fighters attack the Millennium Falcon (Han's home). It sustains heavy damage, but the ship makes it into hyperspace.

The Matrix: Cypher has control of the ship. Everyone else is either dead or connected to the Matrix (i.e., at his mercy), except for Tank. When Cypher is about to kill Neo, he gets fried by Tank, who is alive and wielding the ray gun, now. This stage doubles here as 167 – The Cavalry Arrives and 187 – Ally Is Fine.

Harry Potter: In *The Chamber of Secrets*, someone breaks in and ransacks Harry's dorm in order to steal Tom Riddle's diary.

Sideways: Stephanie learns about Jack imminent wedding, and she goes to the guy's Motel. She breaks Jack's nose with her motorcycle helmet.

Dodgeball: Peter enters his hotel room and finds White in there, waiting to bribe him. Huge Me'Shell comes out of the bathroom, where he just punished the porcelain (the seven-foot-tall man has been having some digestive problems).

Related:
113 – Attack 8: Shock and Awe

133 – Detachment to Protect Allies
The Hero leaves everything and everyone behind.

Description:

The Hero wants to end this and protect friends, so the Hero leaves alone.

It's a noble attitude. But it is also counterphobic; a consequence of the Hero's desperation. It's like when you run into the cold sea instead of going in slowly.

This attitude by the Hero triggers stage 137 – Recrimination by Ally. What the Hero doesn't understand is that the allies are not fighting *for* him: They are fighting *with* him, for what they love. It's their story, too.

Examples:

Star Wars: Luke leaves Dagobah to confront Vader, alone. It's a trap, of course, and he's stepping into it.

The Matrix: Neo prepares his immersion chair: He marches to rescue Morpheus, and he wants to do it alone.

Harry Potter: Hermione petrifies Neville. Ron says, "Sorry. It's for your own good, you know." They leave to find the stone.

Sideways: This stage works more comically: Jack tells Miles to go alone inside Cammi's house and get the wallet, because his ankle hurts.

Dodgeball: Peter vanishes. He doesn't want to tell his friends that he took White's bribe.

Related:

137 – Recrimination by Ally

134 – The Team Gets Scattered
The allies are forced to follow different paths.

Description:

The good guys scatter as a consequence of stage 132 – Attack 9: The Hero's Lair.

That is okay, though; their roles in the final battle will differ, and somehow everyone will end up in the battle station where they are supposed to be.

Examples:

Star Wars: Obi-Wan is gone, Leia is at the Rebel base, Han and Chewie are leaving, and Luke and R2D2 are going to battle.

The Matrix: Dozer, Switch, and Apoc are gone, Morpheus is imprisoned, the Oracle is unreachable, Tank is in the ship, and Neo and Trinity go to battle.

Harry Potter: Dumbledore is gone, Neville is frozen, the other professors are in denial, and the three friends are getting deeper into uncharted territory.

Sideways: Jack is having sex with Cammi, Maya left, Stephanie left, and Miles is alone.

Dodgeball: Patches is gone, Jason is with Amber at the cheerleading tournament, Steve The Pirate wanders alone in the streets, Peter left, and the true "Hero" of the story, the rest of the friends, head to the arena where they will forfeit the game.

Related:
133 – Detachment to Protect Allies

ORDEAL — The Ultimate Hero's Journey — ACT **2.3**

135 – The Hero's Fall
All subplots go south.

Description:

The Hero changed strategies in midpoint, which looked promising. But now Murphy's Law kicks in: Everything that can go wrong does exactly that.

The Hero's reaction depends on the type of hero. Unwilling heroes are either paralyzed or continue moving by inertia; willing heroes keep pushing ahead against all odds.

This is definitely the worst moment for the Hero. The light at the end of the tunnel will be visible in stage 142 – Third Epiphany.

Examples:

Star Wars: The Death Star approaches, Leia is pissed off, Han's gone, and Luke is not that keen about the Force, yet. The chances of survival are infinitesimal—no need to ask C3PO.

The Matrix: The Squids approach, Morpheus's resistance is shaking, half the crew is dead, the ship is about to be destroyed, and Neo believes he is not The One.

Harry Potter: The kids face the "most painful of deaths" by trying to protect the sorcerer's stone. The teachers don't believe the kids' warnings, and advancing gets increasingly difficult and dangerous.

Sideways: Miles's book got rejected again, his ex-wife remarried, the trip is coming to an end, Maya left him in disappointment, and Jack wants to cancel the wedding.

Dodgeball: The game is forfeited, the gym is lost, and Peter is drinking alone at the airport. He has failed his friends and himself.

Related:
142 – Third Epiphany

136 – The Villain Rises
The Villain is closer and closer to the Ultimate Boon.

Description:

The dark side reaches its highest point, and the Hero's arc is at its lowest. The story is headed to end in the worst way.

There is a catch, though: The Hero will soon have a plan. But first the Hero's butt must be kicked into motion (in stage 137 – Recrimination by Ally).

Examples:

Star Wars: The Death Star will soon be in position to fire, after which the movie will be over. Small detail: The Rebels succeeded in extracting the plans from R2D2's memory.

The Matrix: The drugs the Agents gave Morpheus will eventually work. Smith is closer and closer to obtain Zion's codes. Small detail: The Agents ignore that Neo is coming.

Harry Potter: Voldemort entered the room where the sorcerer's stone is hidden. Soon he will be unstoppable. Small detail: Dumbledore put a spell on the stone.

Sideways: Cammi's husband rises. He gets home earlier than expected and catches his wife having sex with Jack, who has to run away naked. The wedding rings (custom-made, irreplaceable) were left there, inside Jack's wallet.

Dodgeball: White bought the gym, won the game, and in minutes he will be given the championship trophy. Small detail: Peter met Lance Armstrong at the Airport, just by chance.

Related:
137 – Recrimination by Ally

137 – Recrimination by Ally

Someone tells the Hero that this is not the way to do things.

Description:

The Hero finds himself in one of two states: Either paralyzed by the overwhelming odds or so obsessed with winning that turning to the dark side is not out of the question. In any case, the Hero is working against the team.

The Hero needs a kick in the rear end. And some ally, who's disappointed in the Hero's attitude, duly obliges.

This recrimination is an emotional call: The Hero must stay true to who he is, and he must trust his friends.

Examples:

Star Wars: Chewie growls at Han for leaving his friends right before the final battle starts. Han answers, "I know what I'm doing!"

The Matrix: Neo wants to rescue Morpheus alone; Trinity tells him to go to hell—she's the ranking officer, so she's coming as well.

Harry Potter: Neville confronts Harry, Ron, and Hermione: "You'll get Gryffindor in trouble again! I... I'll fight you!"

Sideways: Miles tells Jack that going into Cammi's house to get the wallet is a crazy idea. Jack says, "Fuck you, I'll get it myself." He won't.

Dodgeball: Lance Armstrong learns about Peter quitting and tells him, "If people never quit when the going got tough, they'd have nothing to regret all their lives. Good luck to you, Peter. I'm sure this decision won't haunt you forever."

Related:
088 – Good Guys in Disagreement

138 – No Way Back, No Way Forward

The Hero's past is destroyed, and the future is about to be.

Description:

All bonds the Hero had with the Ordinary World are gone. If anything was left of it, in this stage it gets killed or eliminated—a cat, a job, a grandma, whatever. There is no place the Hero can retreat to.

And what is worst, soon the Villain will win this thing and the Hero will have no place left in the world to go to.

Thank god the Hero still has his extraordinary talent.

Examples:

Star Wars: Luke's home is gone, and soon the Empire will destroy his new home, too: the Rebellion. All he has left is the power of the Force. And his friends.

The Matrix: The world Neo knew never existed, and soon the Machines will destroy his future home, Zion, too. All he has left is the power of choice. And his friends.

Harry Potter: In *The Deathly Hallows* movies, Harry has no home to go back to (the Dursleys escaped), and Voldemort is about to destroy Hogwarts. All he has is his magic powers, the loyalty of a wand or two, and his friends.

Sideways: Miles's hopes to get back with Victoria are gone and it looks like he blew his chances with Maya, as well. All he has is one last adventure ahead of him: To get Jack's wallet back.

Dodgeball: Peter gave up the gym, the championship, the girl, and his friends. His past and his future mean nothing. All he has is the bribe money.

Related:

072 – No Going Back

139 – Ticking Clock

This will be over soon.

Description:

Time is the scarcest of commodities: You cannot buy it, and when it's gone, it's gone. This is true for fiction, too. If no clock was set earlier in the story, now is the moment to introduce it.

This is the thing with countdowns: As long as they don't reach zero, everything is okay. So you make sure that the countdown *do* reaches zero, which happens in stage 164 – The Unthinkable Happens.

Now *that's* a climax!

Examples:

Star Wars: We see a computer diagram of the Death Star approaching firing position and a countdown. (It *will* fire.)

The Matrix: The Squids, those murderous machines, where introduced early in the story. Two of them are back, trying to penetrate the Nebuchadnezzar's hull. (They *do* penetrate the hull.)

Harry Potter: If Harry doesn't hurry, Snape is going to reach the chamber where the sorcerer's stone is hidden. (The real villain is Quirrell, who *does* reach the chamber. In fact, he's waiting there for Harry.)

Sideways: The rings are lost, and Jack's wedding is but a few hours away.

Dodgeball: If Peter doesn't arrive soon, his team will have to forfeit the game. (They *do* forfeit the game.)

140 – The Villain's Weakness
The Villain's perfect plan has a teeny-tiny problem.

Description:

Just as the Hero has a Weakness, the Villain has one, too, derived from need and desire.

Now that the Hero knows how the bad guy is going to win this thing, the Hero also knows how to stop him.

Examples:

Star Wars: The Death Star looks invincible, but it has one weakness: One torpedo in the reactor and the whole thing goes *k-boom*. But the Weakness (with capital "W") is Tarkin's: He underestimates the small Rebel attack force; he thinks they are no match for his monstrous battle station.

The Matrix: Smith is invincible. But there is a problem: The Oracle was right. Neo's doubts are gone.

Harry Potter: Voldemort wants to use the stone to return to life. There is a problem, though: Dumbledore's spell. The stone can only be found by someone who wouldn't want to use it, so it magically teleported to Harry's pocket.

Sideways: The wallet is in Cammi's room. Luckily for the guys, Cammi and her husband didn't notice that.

Dodgeball: White Goodman won everything. There is a problem, though: Peter now has $100,000 in cash and a renovated faith in himself.

Related:
171 – The Hero Lets Go

141 – Second Encouragement

The Hero gets a last moment of human intimacy before the ordeal begins.

Description:

This encouragement gives the Hero a reaffirmation of power. It usually comes from the Goddess (or whomever the romantic interest is).

There can be a kiss, a night of love, a word of encouragement, even something as subtle as a look. In any case, the message is "I believe in you."

Examples:

Star Wars: Han tells Luke before the final battle: "May the Force be with you" (no time for romance here).

The Matrix: Neo rescues Trinity from the exploding helicopter, and they embrace in the rooftop.

Harry Potter: There is no romance, but there is a word of encouragement from Hermione. Harry answers, embarrassed, "I'm not as good as you". "Me!," Hermione says. "Books! And cleverness! There are more important things – friendship and bravery and – oh, Harry – be *careful!*"

Sideways: Miles spends the night at Maya's.

Dodgeball: Owen and Fran meet and connect at the bar; romance ensues.

Related:
079 – First Encouragement
169 – Third Encouragement

142 – Third Epiphany

The Hero learns the most important lesson about himself.

Description:

This stage marks the end of the Hero's Weakness. Fighting against it didn't work; the only alternative is to understand it; not to repress the Weakness, but to leave it behind.

This is the last stage of Act 2. Consider ending a chapter here.

Examples:

Star Wars: Luke might not have much faith in the Force, but he hears Obi-Wan's voice again. His distrust starts dissipating.

The Matrix: Neo may not have much belief, but he has the power of choice. And paradoxically, being The One is all about choice.

Harry Potter: Harry might not know much about magic (he is a first-year, after all), but the magic is in him, as he will learn soon.

Sideways: Miles discovers that he has his own agency. "I'm not Jack. I'm just his freshman roommate from San Diego State," he says.

Dodgeball: Peter finds himself with money in his hands (something he always did without) but without friends (something he *never* did without). It's time to turn that around.

Related:
118 – The Ultimate Boon
140 – The Villain's Weakness

FINAL BATTLE — The Ultimate Hero's Journey — ACT 3

143 – Plan C: Infiltrate
No time for explanations.

Description:

The Hero finally has a plan for the final battle. But when asked about it, the Hero only says something cryptic, like "I know what I must do."

One thing is certain: He has factored self-sacrifice into the equation.

Examples:

Star Wars: Luke retracts his targeting computer. When he's asked what's wrong, he only answers: "Nothing, I'm all right."

The Matrix: Tank asks Neo, "What do you need, besides a miracle?" He only answers, "Guns. Lots of guns."

Harry Potter: Harry discovered which one of the flying keys opens the door they must open in order to continue ahead. Hermione asks, "What's wrong, Harry?" He only answers, "It's too simple."

Sideways: Miles and Jack discuss how to recover the wallet. Miles only says, "Hold on," and leaves the car.

Dodgeball: Peter shows up at the game. Everyone looks at him, waiting for an explanation. He just says, "What? I got a plan."

Related:
064 – Plan A: Let Events Unfold
120 – Plan B: Rescue
126 – The Villain's Stronghold
140 – The Villain's Weakness

144 – The Reluctant Aid

A character with some special power reluctantly helps.

Description:

The Hero recruits the help of a character who is essentially neutral. This character doesn't care about the Hero's quest, nor about the dark side. The Reluctant Aid agrees to help, but for a price.

This character doesn't become part of the team but remains reclusive and independent. The Aid is beyond good and evil and seems unaffected by the world's problems.

After this scene, the Reluctant Aid disappears from the story.

Examples:

Star Wars: In *Episode I - The Phantom Menace,* Watto releases Anakin in exchange for money.

The Matrix: In the sequel, *The Matrix Reloaded,* Persephone gives Neo the Keymaker in exchange for one true kiss.

Harry Potter: In *The Deathly Hallows - Part 2,* Helena Ravenclaw reluctantly reveals the location of her mother's diadem only after Harry promises that he will destroy the object.

Sideways: (Not applicable).

Dodgeball: The help comes from none other than Chuck Norris. The destiny of Average Joe's is in his hands—literally: He gives the thumbs-up, and Average Joe's can play despite having forfeited the game. So much for neutrality.

Related:

081 – The False Enemy
083 – The Random Ally

145 – The Comedic Relief
Something funny happens.

Description:

As a Joker stage, the Comedic Relief can be placed wherever you need it, but it has more effect after something has gone downhill.

Humor is important, no matter the genre. This stage reminds us to not take ourselves too seriously, and it reminds the audience that this is supposed to be entertaining.

It only takes one funny word or situation not to write a totally humorless story.

Examples:

Star Wars: C3PO is in charge of funny remarks, but the best comedic situation is delivered by Han Solo, posing as a mild-mannered stormtrooper: "Uh... We had a slight weapons malfunction, but, uh... everything's perfectly all right now. We're fine, thank you. How are you?"

The Matrix: I believe this would be the perfect movie if it had just a pinch of humor somewhere. The closest to it is Mouse's monologue about the Woman in the Red Dress.

Harry Potter: Potions explode, Uncle Vernon's disgusting sister inflates like a balloon and floats away, and candy has earwax's flavor. Harry's stories are full of funny situations.

Sideways: This is a drama, but many scenes have a funny side: Jack scares bullies away with a golf club, men run around stark naked, etc.

Dodgeball: This movie is all about comedic situations, of course. And it has one moment of drama (see stage 135 – The Hero's Fall), which is exactly what every good comedy needs.

146 – Sword Upgrade
The Hero gets a more powerful weapon.

Description:

The acquisition of a new "sword" (a weapon, tool, or instrument) is a symbol of the ascending Hero's arc.

There is a personal relationship with the weapon the Hero uses. It either belonged to an ancestor (like *Andúril*, Aragorn's sword in *The Lord of The Rings*), or was received by divine right (Excalibur), or was forged by the Hero (like Luke's new lightsaber).

Examples:

Star Wars: Luke starts using his father's lightsaber, but a Jedi must build his own. He does, and Vader says, examining the weapon: "Your skills are complete." For the coming battle, however, he will be using something bigger: An Incom T-65B X-wing Starfighter, with torpedoes and everything.

The Matrix: Neo goes from using "lots of guns" to using none at all—*that's* his upgrade.

Harry Potter: Harry uses several wands: Ollivander's wand, a snatcher's wand that Ron gave him, Draco's wand, and the Elder Wand—the most powerful in existence. He destroys that last one, though, a symbol of staying true to himself.

Sideways: Miles doesn't use any weapons (just like Neo), but only his wits.

Dodgeball: No weapons upgrade here, either—just uniform upgrades.

Related:

056 – Presentation of the Sword
173 – Emergence of the Sword

147 – Suit Up and Go
Both sides get armed to the teeth.

Description:

Both Hero and Villain wear their Sunday suits in preparation for the final battle. Once again, the external appearance is indicative of an internal resolution.

Both suits (the Hero's and the Villain's) come with an ace up the sleeve, but those remain secret until the Climax.

Examples:

Star Wars: Luke wears a pilot's suit; R2D2 is placed in Luke's ship, and all fighters are fueled, armed, and ready. In the Death Star, there is no shortage of shiny uniforms, of course—or ships, or weapons.

The Matrix: The Agents' suits always look like they were just picked up from the cleaners, no matter if they just punched their way through a concrete wall. Neo and Trinity wear the coolest outfits that anyone can code.

Harry Potter: The kids, usually in school uniforms, dress in normal clothes for the final mission.

Sideways: After running naked for five miles dodging mean ostriches, Jack puts some clothes on.

Dodgeball: The guys, wearing their yellow uniforms, take position in the field.

Related:
065 – New Clothes

148 – Rallying the Troops
A figure of authority delivers a pep talk.

Description:

Epic tales feature several troop rallies; in other genres, this stage can be just a simple, intimate conversation. The key is to inspire the warriors by talking about values they are fighting for. It has to be a short but powerful speech.

Examples:

Star Wars: Luke's call is made to Han, asking for his help in the final battle. The speech succeeds, but not immediately (right now, Han leaves the Rebel base with his money. He doesn't want to take part in the final battle).

The Matrix: Neo tells Trinity and Tank that he believes in something: He believes he can bring Morpheus back.

Harry Potter: Giant magical chess. Ron encourages Harry to finish the game, and to continue. "Do you want to stop Snape or not? Harry, it's you that has to go on. I know it. Not me, not Hermione—you."

Sideways: Jack directs Miles to Cammi's house: "Yeah, this is the block. Just keep going." Their final battle is to recover the wallet with the rings.

Dodgeball: Peter's pep talk starts with the question, "What's our motto?" The team replies, "Aim low." "That's right, " Peter says. "All I'm asking is that you give it your best for Patches. I say we go out there, let it all hang loose, try to have some fun. I mean, it's only dodgeball, right?" It's not "just dodgeball", of course, but his words reveal that he is already letting go, a foreshadowing of stage 171.

Related:
122 – The Hero Leads
171 - The Hero Lets Go

FINAL BATTLE   The Ultimate Hero's Journey   ACT **3**

149 – The Villain's Grand Entrance
It's David versus Goliath all over again.

Description:

Welcome to the Villain's inner cave, his natural element, the place where the Villain is most powerful.

This place shows the antagonists in all their glory, reflecting their true personality—think Dracula's Castle or Mount Doom.

Examples:

Star Wars: The Imperial forces are intimidating, an immense evil armada. Only a handful of small Rebel fighters stands in its way.

The Matrix: Security guards, SWAT, policemen, the Agents—Neo and Trinity march to face them all.

Harry Potter: Quirrell stands up straight, and he doesn't stutter anymore. He looks powerful and evil. And he has Voldemort living inside his body. Scary.

Sideways: Miles looks Lilliputian compared to Cammi's husband, a naked behemoth screaming obscenities against a background of heavy metal music.

Dodgeball: Globo Gym players are huge, muscular, and have names like "Laser, Blazer, Taser, and all kinds of 'asers."

Related:
150 – Humble Entrance of the Hero

150 – Humble Entrance of the Hero

This Hero enters the place where everything is going to end.

Description:

The Hero is the underdog, always outnumbered and outgunned. The only hope is to outsmart the Villain.

The entrance of the Hero is humble but radiates self-confidence. The Hero fights for something bigger than himself.

Every piece of the board is in position, and both Hero and Villain are ready to fight. All the events of the story have fatally driven them to this place and time.

Examples:

Star Wars: Thirty single-pilot Rebel ships feel the gravity shake as they enter the Death Star space. They unfold their wings, locking them in the "X" attack position.

The Matrix: Security checkpoint. Neo opens his coat and shows the astonished guards all the weapons he carries.

Harry Potter: Harry walks into the secret room where the sorcerer's stone is kept hidden. Professor Quirrell is already there.

Sideways: Miles enters Cammi's house through the back door and advances on all fours toward the bedroom.

Dodgeball: Peter enters the field while jogging confidently. The final game is about to begin.

Related:
149 – The Villain's Grand Entrance

151 – The Villain's Monologue
The Villain tries to convert the Hero to the dark side.

Description:

The Villain offers a deal: Join me and there will be peace; surrender, and I'll make sure you obtain everything you desire.

This promise sounds not only reasonable, but also tempting. The deal includes a malignant requirement, of course: All contracts with the Devil are like that.

If the offer is rejected, apocalypse will ensue.

Examples:

Star Wars: In *Episode V*, Darth Vader asks Luke to join him. Together they can defeat the Emperor and bring peace to the Galaxy. The condition: Luke must become a Sith, or else everyone dies.

The Matrix: In *Reloaded,* the Architect tells Neo that he can stop the attack and restart Zion with a handful of selected people, if he goes through *that* door. The condition: Everyone else in Zion must die, including Trinity. Or else, everyone dies.

Harry Potter: Voldemort says, "Tell me, Harry, would you like to see your mother and father again? Together, we can bring them back." The condition: Harry has to hand over the sorcerer's stone.

Sideways: Jack proposes Miles that they should move to the wine county; they could buy a vineyard, they could design their own wine, and Miles could write a new novel. It sounds nice. The condition: Throw the wedding (and Christine) out the window.

Dodgeball: White bribes Peter: One hundred thousand dollars in exchange for the gym and the game.

Related:
128 – The Villain's Speech

152 – Temptation Rejected

The Villain promises to destroy everything the Hero loves.

Description:

At the core of all evil there is a fascist imposition: It's either the Villain's way or the morgue's way.

When presented with this cursed choice, the Hero doesn't talk much; Evil cannot be reasoned with. Instead, the Hero waits for the moment to act.

Examples:

Star Wars: In *Episode VI – Return of the Jedi*, Darth Vader says "peace," but he means total destruction of any opposition. Luke doesn't answer and stays in hiding, waiting for the right moment.

The Matrix: Neo rejects the Architect's bait and chooses to go through the second door, instead. He chooses to save Trinity, not Humanity. No previous "One" did such a thing before.

Harry Potter: Harry screams one word: "Liar!"

Sideways: Miles sees through Jack's delusion about leaving it all behind and moving to the wine county. He tells Jack, "You're crazy. You've gone crazy."

Dodgeball: Rejection? Nah. Peter already took the money.

Related:

033 – Attack 3: The Hero Resists
101 – The Temptress

FINAL BATTLE — The Ultimate Hero's Journey — ACT 3

153 – Back to the Hook

The Hook *described a future ordeal. Now that ordeal begins.*

Description:

This moment is like the highest point after the steady climb of a roller coaster: Now the last and most exhilarating part of the ride begins.

This stage tells the audience, "Okay, that's what happened until right now. Now let's find out how it's going to end."

This is a Joker stage; it can be placed wherever works best, but always here in Act 3.

Examples:

Star Wars: The first scene showed the Empire chasing the Rebels; now we get back to that same "David versus Goliath" symbolism: The meager squadron of Rebel fighters against the mighty Imperial Fleet.

The Matrix: The movie started with a computer screen cracking a phone number; in its last scene the same screen comes back—only this time it shows the message "System Error."

Harry Potter: The first sequence in the film showed Harry's scar. Now we see it again; it hurts because of Voldemort's presence.

Bonus Examples:

The Lord of the Rings: The action starts in the Shire and ends in the Shire.

Crimson Tide: This movie starts on an aircraft carrier, and it goes back to the same carrier just before the final scene.

Notting Hill: This movie starts with Will walking down Portobello Road. Before the "final battle" we see him in the same situation.

Related:

001 – The Hook

154 – Battle against Major Guardians
The final battle starts.

Description:

The Hero will get to the Final Boss but must first get past the dark side's most powerful lieutenants.

Examples:

Star Wars: The Rebels fight their way through the laser turrets and the TIE Fighters—the Guardians of the Death Star. The legendary battle of Yavin has begun.

The Matrix: Neo and Trinity fight a SWAT team—the Guardians of the building. The scene that ensues (the shooting in the lobby) has a place among the most spectacular action sequences ever filmed.

Harry Potter: Quirrell (Voldemort's Guardian) and Harry fight for the sorcerer's stone.

Sideways: Miles's final battle: Outrunning the humongous tow-truck driver—the Guardian of the wedding rings.

Dodgeball: The fearsome Purple Cobras (the Guardians of the trophy) deliver a painful ordeal of flying balls.

Related:

156 – Battling Styles
157 – Allies out of Combat

155 – Attack 10: Furious Chase

May the dance of death begin.

Description:

The Hero makes a move, and the dark side shows its terrifying power. Objective: Catch and destroy.

Examples:

Star Wars: The X-wings start the attack, moving across a storm of lasers.

The Matrix: Neo is in the building. Smith is furious; Thomas Anderson must die. Now.

Harry Potter: Harry tries to escape; Quirrell chases him.

Sideways: Cammi's and her husband are making love in the bedroom as Miles grabs the wallet from the dresser and runs away. The chase starts.

Dodgeball: The Cobras are too powerful. Globo Gym is dominating the game.

156 – Battling Styles

The Hero fights with a virtuous attitude; the Villain doesn't.

Description:

The Hero uses cleverness, agility, and courage; the Villain uses deception, tricks, brute force, and trash talk—all indications that the Villain can't leave narcissism behind. And that is precisely the reason why the Villain is going to be defeated.

Examples:

Star Wars: Luke helps his comrades, who are pinned down by enemy fighters. Vader and Tarkin talk about how magnificent this day is: It has seen the end of Obi-Wan Kenobi, and now it will see the end of the Rebellion.

The Matrix: Neo and Trinity cover for each other, always putting themselves into harm's way. As the chase continues in the streets, the Agents shoot at them in the middle of a market full of people, not caring about anything or anyone.

Harry Potter: Voldemort is the most powerful dark wizard ever, and he uses intimidation and lies; Harry does whatever he can—he is just eleven, after all.

Sideways: Miles wants to get back his friend's rings; Cammi's husband wants blood.

Dodgeball: White Goodman cheats during the play (stepping on the line, throwing balls to players not in play, etc.) He yells Gordon, "You're out, four-eyes!," which is just a token of his constant trash talking.

Related:
154 – Battle against Major Guardians
157 – Allies out of Combat

157 – Allies out of Combat
The good guys are eliminated one by one.

Description:

The forces of evil are strong. They eliminate (although not necessarily kill) the Hero's companions, one by one. The Hero has to be the only one left who can meet the Villain hand-to-hand.

The clock continues ticking.

Examples:

Star Wars: One by one, the Rebel fighters are destroyed. The leader of the Rebel squadron misses the shot, and then his ship is destroyed. Luke must attempt the shot himself. The Death Star is closer and closer to Yavin. R2D2 gets blasted by an enemy.

The Matrix: Morpheus and Trinity were extracted from the Matrix, but Neo couldn't get out. He must face Smith alone inside The Matrix. The Squids attack the ship in the real world.

Harry Potter: Harry faces Quirrell and Voldemort alone, because Ron and Hermione could not get past the chamber's tests.

Sideways: Miles had to go alone, because Jack has a sprained ankle and is unable to run, or even walk.

Dodgeball: One by one, Peter's teammates are eliminated. He ends up facing White Goodman and Me'Shell alone.

Related:
154 – Battle against Major Guardians
156 – Battling Styles

158 – Run for Your Life (3)

The Villain gains momentum. The Hero avoids the blows.

Description:

Deadly, brutal attacks. The Hero cannot oppose resistance or fight back. Dodge, escape, and hide are the only options available.

Just as the Hero started the trials winning and then losing in the descending arc of Act 2, here the Hero starts losing and works his way up to victory.

Examples:

Star Wars: Luke dodges the deadly lasers and maneuvers across the Death Star's surface. His companions fall under enemy fire around him.

The Matrix: Neo dodges bullets and punches, and eventually he has to run away to find a hardline telephone in order to escape the Matrix. He is surrounded by the Agents.

Harry Potter: Harry tries to escape, but the evil professor flies through the room and catches the kid.

Sideways: Miles runs all the way to the car, one step ahead of Cammi's husband.

Dodgeball: Peter dodges the fast balls thrown at him, just barely escaping.

Related:

110 – Run for Your Life (1)
123 – Run for Your Life (2)

159 – The Oblivious Innocent
Some character has no idea what's going on.

Description:

The universe as we know it may be coming to an end, but somewhere some minor character is going about daily business, oblivious to the battle. Children are the archetypical figure of the innocent.

Just like stage 145 – The Comedic Relief, this is a Joker stage that dissipates some tension and reminds the audience that they should be having fun. I include it here, but you place it wherever it better serves your story.

Examples:

Star Wars: (Not applicable).

The Matrix: (Not applicable).

Harry Potter: In *Harry Potter and The Deathly Hallows,* Ron, Hermione, and Harry are sitting at a coffee bar. Two vicious Death Eaters arrive, and the shooting starts. We see the waitress working back in the kitchen, listening to music with headphones on, oblivious to the terrible fight happening a few feet away.

Sideways: A young boy hears Jack cursing. His father tells Jack to watch this mouth.

Dodgeball: White Goodman hits the soda cup of a boy passing by. White also takes a sandwich from to another boy's hands and brutally eats it. It's official: White is a total jerk.

Related:

098 – The Awkward Innocent

160 – A Cross of Swords
The Hero and the Villain collide.

Description:

The Hero and the Villain close on each other in combat.

The violent confrontation and the physical contact represent the circularity, unity, and opposition of Good and Evil.

The Villain gets the upper hand.

Examples:

Star Wars: Vader shoots down Luke's wingmen and says, "The Force is strong with this one."

The Matrix: Smith grabs Neo from the neck and immobilizes him.

Harry Potter: Quirrell grabs Harry and immobilizes him.

Sideways: Cammi's husband hits Miles's car.

Dodgeball: What more physical can contact get than a rubber ball thrown to your face?

Related:
157 – Allies out of Combat

161 – At the Mercy of the Villain
The battle goes wrong for the Hero.

Description:

Well, the Hero has to die. Otherwise, where is the sacrifice?

The Hero is immobilized, conscious but hurt.

The Villain is mostly unharmed and ready to deliver the final blow.

Examples:

Star Wars: Vader has Luke's ship in his sights. He has a missile lock, now, and a clean shot.

The Matrix: Smith has Neo pinned down on the subway tracks. A train approaches at full speed.

Harry Potter: Quirrell has Harry pinned down on the floor.

Sideways: Jack and Miles are trapped inside the car, and Cammi's husband is trying to open it.

Dodgeball: Peter eliminates Me'Shell but is left exposed to White's shot. Here comes the ball.

Related:

164 – The Unthinkable Happens

162 – Death Foretold

The Villain tell the Hero, "You are going to die now."

Description:

These words from the Villain sound like a farewell, but it's just mock sadness—the caricature of a magnanimous victor.

The Hero doesn't talk much, though. The Hero knows what's coming: Unavoidable sacrifice. Why talk?

Examples:

Star Wars: Vader says, "I have you now." One push of the trigger and Luke's dead. Luke says nothing and flies directly to his target.

The Matrix: Smith says, "Do you hear that, Mr. Anderson? That is the sound of inevitability. That is the sound of your death. Goodbye, Mr. Anderson."

Harry Potter: Voldemort orders Quirrell: "Kill him!"

Sideways: Cammi's husband screams, "You motherfuckers! I'll kill you!"

Dodgeball: White says, "Goodbye, Peter. I always knew you were weak."

Related:

163 – The Hero's Death
166 – The Hero's Resurrection

FINAL BATTLE — The Ultimate Hero's Journey — ACT 3

163 – The Hero's Death

The Hero dies (either literally or symbolically).

Description:

The Hero gives up life for the quest.

The problem is that, by dying now, the quest fails. So this is the worst of endings.

In fact, if the story were a tragedy, this would be the end. In a bittersweet story, the Hero would die, but at least the good side's object would be achieved (e.g., *Aliens 4,* and *Elysium*). But a story with a happy ending must continue.

Examples:

Star Wars: Vader opens fire on Luke's ship. There's no escape.

The Matrix: Neo opens the door of the apartment where the phone is already ringing. Smith is standing inside. He repeatedly shoots Neo in the chest. Neo dies.

Harry Potter: Quirrell chokes Harry. No one can save him now.

Sideways: Miles tries to start the car. One more bang on the car window and it's going to break.

Dodgeball: White launches a fast ball and hits Peter. Peter is eliminated.

Related:
162 – Death Foretold
166 – The Hero's Resurrection

164 – The Unthinkable Happens

The worst happens (or it looks like it does).

Description:

A total shock.

The audience thought, "Of course, that is never going to happen." And then, BAM—it happens.

Don't paint yourself into a corner, though. Make sure you have a clever way to revert the catastrophe; avoid having to resort to a *deus-ex-machina*, i.e., an utterly improbable, illogical or baseless plot twist that conveniently solves the problem. No: The Hero—and the audience—must be convinced that everything is lost.

Examples:

Star Wars: The Death Star finally gets in position. Tarkin gives the order to shoot. It's all over.

The Matrix: How can Neo be dead? He is The One—isn't he?

Harry Potter: Quirrell is killing Harry, and the sorcerer's stone falls from Harry's hand. The kid is lost, and Voldemort has immortality within reach.

Sideways: Miles learns that his ex-wife not only remarried but is also pregnant. Every hope he had to get back together evaporates. We hear the voice of one of Miles's students reading a passage from *A Separate Peace* that narrates a death. Life as he knows it is over.

Dodgeball: Average Joe's loses the game. The dream is over. White Goodman falls on his knees, crying tears of joy.

FINAL BATTLE — The Ultimate Hero's Journey — ACT **3**

165 – Emergence of the Elixir
"Oh, right, that gizmo from the beginning!"

Description:

The Elixir doesn't work like the "shark repellent" that Adam West's Batman just happen to have in his utility belt. No, this artifact was given to the Hero back in stage 069, remember? It is the thing the Hero put in a pocket and we all forgot about.

In many movies, however, the Elixir is not an artifact but a person or an emotion. In this case, the one who revives the Hero is either the Goddess or the closest sidekick.

Examples:

Star Wars: The Millennium Falcon ("that piece of junk") is Luke's Elixir. Laser shots from high orbit rain on Vader's ship. Han is back!

The Matrix: Trinity's love is Neo's Elixir. The Oracle told her that she was to fall in love with The One. Trinity says, "I love you, Neo. So, you see, you can't be dead."

Harry Potter: Harry's Elixir is the love and magic powers he received from his mother. In an effort to breathe, Harry takes Quirrell's hand from his neck, and the dark wizard's hand turns into crumbling, black ash.

Sideways: Miles's Elixir is his answering machine (see next stages). But for this particular scene his Elixir is his old Saab; there he finds refuge from the attack of the big boss of this movie.

Dodgeball: The referee saw that White overstepped the line in his last shot. Double fault. The game is not over yet.

Related:

069 – Presentation of the Elixir

166 – The Hero's Resurrection

It's not over until it's over.

Description:

The Hero comes back to life.

Examples:

Star Wars: (see next stage, 167 – The Cavalry Arrives)

The Matrix: Neo's heart starts beating again.

Harry Potter: Harry stands up and faces Quirrell again.

Sideways: Miles's car starts and the friends can escape from the attack.

Dodgeball: The ADAA Rule Book saves the good guys again. It's Continuation Rule 113-D, sir. We are about to witness the greatest happening in sports: Sudden-death Dodgeball!

Related:

163 – The Hero's Death
176 – Resurrection of the Villain

167 – The Cavalry Arrives

The Hero receives help from an unexpected ally.

Description:

This stage marks the return of a human Elixir—someone we met before but who we almost forgot. This character (usually the False Enemy, more rarely the Reluctant Aid or the Oblivious Innocent) saves the Hero from certain death.

This stage poses a challenge for authors, because this help has to be both foreshadowed (to avoid *deus-ex-machina*) and unexpected (so it creates surprise).

Examples:

Star Wars: Han attacks Vader, who loses control of his fighter.

The Matrix: This happens later on, when Neo has already won the final battle against the Agents. Tank guides Neo to the closest hardline phone. Only then will Morpheus be able to trigger the EMP to kill the Squids that are destroying the Nebuchadnezzar.

Harry Potter: In *The Sorcerer's Stone* there is no Cavalry—Harry deals with Quirrell alone. In *The Deathly Hallows*, the Cavalry is Neville; he decapitates Nagini, the last of Voldemort's horcruxes, just when the murderous serpent is about to kill Ron and Hermione.

Sideways: Miles presses the answering machine's play button and hears, "Hello, Miles—it's Maya." She is The Cavalry, who "saves" Miles with her call.

Dodgeball: The Referee is The Cavalry here. White protests, but the referee's judgment is final.

Related:

081 – The False Enemy
144 – The Reluctant Aid
187 – Ally Is Fine

168 – Second Declaration of Love

They are one step closer to that kiss.

Description:

The attraction is clear now. However, the lovers cannot come together yet, because of the ticking clock.

This is another step in the romantic subplot, which concludes in stage 185 – Consummation of Love.

Examples:

Star Wars: (Not applicable, because the love story between Han and Leia develops across several movies).

The Matrix: See 166 – The Hero's Resurrection.

Harry Potter: (Not applicable. Since the characters are children, yet, the romantic subplots develop across several movies).

Sideways: Miles is the one doing the love declaration, albeit a sad one: He leaves a sincere farewell message for Maya before going back to Los Angeles: "This has been a big deal for me... I really like you, Maya."

Dodgeball: This happens when Kate is eliminated. When she leaves the playing field, she stretches out her hand and touches Peter's. White Goodman, jealous, hits her in the face with a ball.

Related:
124 – First Declaration of Love
185 – Consummation of Love

169 – Third Encouragement

The Hero gets encouragement to go ahead and finish it.

Description:

Someone (usually the Goddess, but not necessarily) either gives a word of encouragement to the Hero, or calls the Hero to action.

Examples:

Star Wars: Han says, "You're all clear, kid. Now let's blow this thing and go home."

The Matrix: Trinity orders Neo, "Now, get up!"

Harry Potter: Before getting killed by Voldemort in *The Deathly Hallows*, Harry's parents appear to him and say, "We will be with you, always."

Sideways: Maya's message tells Miles to let her know if he plans to get back to Buellton sometime, encouraging him to return and see her.

Dodgeball: Kate leaves the field with her face hurting from White's last illegal shot. She tells Peter, "Kick his ass."

Related:
079 – First Encouragement
141 – Second Encouragement

170 – Right Words at the Right Time (2)

The words that caused the Hero's first epiphany resonate again.

Description:

Weapons, talismans, and swords: Those are just objects that help the Hero's quest; the real key to victory is the Hero's enlightenment, and the Right Words are the vessel.

Examples:

Star Wars: Obi-Wan's voice returns: "Let go, Luke. Trust the Force."

The Matrix: Neo remembers the words "There is no spoon." The Matrix is an illusion, so he doesn't have to be bound by it.

Sideways: "The day you open a '61 Cheval Blanc, that's the special occasion," Maya once told Miles. He opens the bottle. Life itself is a special occasion, isn't it?

Dodgeball: Patches's apparition on the scarf tells Peter, "Listen up, crotch stain. Remember your training and trust your instincts. I believe in you."

Bonus Examples:

The Lord of The Rings: The Right Words are Gandalf's: "All we have to decide is what to do with the time that is given us." Frodo didn't choose to be the Ring Bearer, but he decides to take the Ring to Mordor and destroy it.

Spiderman: "With great power comes great responsibility," says Uncle Ben, words that resonate in Peter Parker's mind, inspiring him to become a superhero.

Related:

061 – First Epiphany
097 – Right Words at the Right Time (1)
119 – Second Epiphany

| APOTHEOSIS | The Ultimate Hero's Journey | ACT **3** |

142 – Third Epiphany

171 – The Hero Lets Go
The Weakness is transcended.

Description:

Reality forced the Hero to assume his true self. The Hero must stop fighting the weakness and simply transcend it, taking a leap of faith.

Examples:

Star Wars: This will be over in seconds. The Death Star starts its firing sequence. Taking such shot without a targeting computer is impossible, but Luke advances toward the exhaust port at full speed, anyway.

The Matrix: How can Neo be dead if he is The One? Answer: He can't. The Oracle told him, "*Temet Nosce*" ("know thyself"), and now he realizes that his weakness is imaginary. He stands up and faces the Agents again.

Harry Potter: Harry embodies virtues, mainly courage and loyalty; he doesn't have Weaknesses, per se. He, like Frodo Baggins, just keeps going.

Sideways: Miles becomes a better man by *being* a better man (a role that transcends that of the wedding). Defeatism, depression, and touchiness—all has to be left behind.

Dodgeball: Peter's indolence took him nowhere in life; it is clear now that not deciding anything is a decision, too—and not the best one.

Related:
026 – The Hero's Weakness

172 – The Hero's Verbal Attack
The Hero undermines the Villain's self-confidence.

Description:

Words have power; they are weapons targeted to the mind.

Another psychological attack happens, but this time, the Hero is the one taking the offensive. The Hero says something that throws the Villain off balance.

Examples:

Star Wars: This happens when Luke hears a joyous scream through the communicator: "Yahoo!" Then Han destroys Vader's wingmen and throws Vader's ship off orbit.

The Matrix: The Agents empty their clips at Neo. He says, "No," and the bullets stop in midair, right in front of him, under the astonished looks of the Agents.

Harry Potter: In *The Deathly Hallows*, Harry grabs Voldemort by the neck and tells him, face to face, "Come on, Tom. Let's end this the way we started it: Together." Voldemort screams in anger and horror as Harry drags him down the abyss. By calling him "Tom," Harry breaks the fear that the name "Voldemort" inspires, and also reminds the Villain that, deep down, he is just Tom—a scared little boy.

Sideways: The Wedding. The words are the priest's, who is pronouncing the marriage. Miles and Jack peek at each other and smile. Their old selves are defeated, and they both emerge from the ceremony as new men.

Dodgeball: Peter tells White, "You look awful fat in those pants." White Goodman's obesity complex comes back with a vengeance.

Related:

073 – The Hero's Determination
174 – The Hero Is Unstoppable

173 – Emergence of the Sword
The Hero launches the final attack.

Description:

The Sword symbolizes the power to defeat evil. The Hero brandish this weapon and advances to finish the battle.

Examples:

Star Wars: Luke feels the Force. Not even Vader can stop him now. He is ready to shoot.

The Matrix: Neo takes one bullet and lets it fall to the floor. The other bullets fall as well. He can change the Matrix as he sees fit.

Harry Potter: Harry grabs Quirrell's face. The dark wizard starts turning to ash from head to toe.

Sideways: Miles's "sword" is his newfound self-confidence. He decides to go for Maya.

Dodgeball: Peter's "sword" is a beautiful silver dodgeball, ready to be shot.

Related:

056 – Presentation of the Sword
146 – Sword Upgrade

174 – The Hero Is Unstoppable

Apotheosis approaches—and your body knows it.

Description:

You can feel it in your stomach: The Hero is going to win. You can see the serenity and determination.

In movies, this feeling is almost subliminally transmitted by music. In a novel, it has to be done with text—or better yet, with subtext.

Examples:

Star Wars: Luke uses the Force and fires the explosive charges into the exhaust port.

The Matrix: Neo sees everything around him constructed in the Matrix's code. Smith attacks furiously, but Neo easily controls him with one hand, without even looking at the Agent.

Harry Potter: In *The Sorcerer's Stone,* Quirrell's whole body crumbles as he continues walking toward Harry. In *The Deathly Hallows,* the Elder Wand leaves Voldemort's hand and flies to Harry's. The Dark Lord is on his knees.

Sideways: Miles drives to Maya's home, while we still hear her voice in the background.

Dodgeball: Peter rubs his fingers, his senses at maximum alert. He stands serene and confident. The world disappears.

Related:

073 – The Hero's Determination
172 – The Hero's Verbal Attack

175 – The Villain "Dies"

It's the Villain's turn to go down.
The Villain is dead. For sure. Right?

Description:

Because the death of the Villain is the most cathartic stage, it usually happens twice. This is the first of those times.

The Villain's death provides satisfaction to the audience, but also leaves them wondering if the Villain is really gone (hint: he's not).

Examples:

Star Wars: Vader's ship was shot out of the sky. What happened to him?

The Matrix: With one kick, Neo sends Smith flying across the hall. Neo wins the fight, but is Smith dead?

Harry Potter: Quirrell disintegrates on the floor, but what happened to Voldemort?

Sideways: (Not applicable).

Dodgeball: Peter's shot catches White in the stomach, sending him flying backward across the field. Peter wins the tournament. White is done, right?

Related:

177 – Apotheosis

176 – Resurrection of the Villain

This guy doesn't know the word "quit".

Description:

The Villain may have lost the Boon, the battle, the girl, everything—but he's not done yet. The Villain comes back to life and launches a last, desperate, furious attack.

Examples:

Star Wars: Vader is not dead; he regains control of his ship.

The Matrix: Smith stands up. His sunglasses are gone (a symbol of his defeat). But he is not done yet.

Harry Potter: Voldemort's dark spirit flies through Harry's body, as if he wanted to kill the boy. Harry falls backward, unconscious.

Sideways: (Not applicable).

Dodgeball: "What are you so happy about, La Fleur? None of this matters," says White with scorn. "You signed your gym over to me last night, remember? You lost. I won. Suck failure, freaks."

Related:
175 – The Villain "Dies"
177 – Apotheosis

177 – Apotheosis
The Villain is gone, this time for good.

Description:

The Villain finally dies, is imprisoned, is ridiculed, or simply escapes, should you need this Villain for your next novel.

The final battle is over, and the Hero acquires the Ultimate Boon.

Examples:

Star Wars: The explosive charges detonate and the Death Star is destroyed in a magnificent explosion. Vader escapes.

The Matrix: Neo enters Smith's body and destroys him from the inside in a magnificent explosion.

Harry Potter: In *The Deathly Hallows,* Voldemort is destroyed in a magnificent explosion.

Sideways: Miles knocks on Maya's door; such is the apotheosis in this story. It's so simple and powerful that the movie ends right here, a second before Miles's definitive triumph happens (i.e., Maya opening that door, which we never get to see). Extraordinary.

Dodgeball: Personnel from the Las Vegas casino make their way among the public and present Peter with his winnings: Five million dollars. He bet the bribe money, which allows him to buy the controlling stock of Globo Gym, and consequently Average Joe's, too. Peter tells White, "You're fired, pal." White explodes in a fit of rage and has to be escorted out of the arena.

Related:
179 – Master of Two Worlds

178 – Lieutenants Vanish

After their boss is out, the dark side's lieutenants run away.

Description:

Fighting to the last man is a mark of Heroism—something the antagonist doesn't have. The Villain's lieutenants run for the hills.

This is an additional catharsis. It reinforces the previous one (the death of the Villain) and underlines the light side's victory.

Examples:

Star Wars: The Empire has lost, and the remainder of the Imperial fleet gets disbanded.

The Matrix: After Smith explodes, Agents Brown and Jones look at each other in disbelief. Then they run away.

Harry Potter: in *The Deathly Hallows*, after Voldemort dies, the Death Eaters run away scared.

Sideways: (Not applicable).

Dodgeball: The rest of the Purples Cobras follow White out of the field, trying to calm him down.

179 – Master of Two Worlds
The Hero's highest moment of glory.

Description:

The Hero defeated the Villain (a symbol of the Adventure World) and defeated the Hero's own defective self (a symbol of the Ordinary World). The Hero has transcended death, and a supernatural aura surrounds the Hero.

Here is evident that the Hero acquired the Boon; however, usually there is another reward that goes beyond the expected winnings.

Note that nothing is said in this stage: The Hero just shines.

Examples:

Star Wars: Luke exhales, relieved, in his cockpit. He achieved victory as a pilot of the Rebellion. But he also started his path as a Jedi. There are two literal worlds here: Yavin and the Death Star, and Luke won in both of them.

The Matrix: Neo inhales and exhales, and the Matrix curves around him. There are two worlds here: The real world and the simulated world, and Neo mastered both of them.

Harry Potter: Harry saves both worlds: The magic world and the muggle world. He is now also the owner of the Deathly Hallows (the Invisibility Cloak, the Resurrection Stone, and the Alder Wand), and the most powerful wizard ever.

Sideways: Miles won in both the world of friendship (in relation to Jack) and the world of love (in relation to Maya). But more than anything, he triumphed over himself.

Dodgeball: Peter won both in the sports world and in the business world: He won the tournament and the $50,000. But he also won the five million dollars, the girl, and the girl's girl (please, spare me the explanation).

180 – Celebration

The order in the world is restored.

Description:

In some stories, the ordeal is so intense that an all-out party would feel out of place. However, there is always at least a subtle hint of celebration—a smile, a physical show of relief, something.

In any case, this stage shows whatever is left of the winning team, and also remembers those who were lost.

Examples:

Star Wars: The Rebellion wins. People in the Rebel base cheer and hug.

The Matrix: Humanity wins. There is no cheering (too many have died). Celebration symbolism: Fireworks-like sparks all around them, in the ship.

Harry Potter: In *The Deathly Hallows*, Hogwarts wins. There is no cheering (too many have been lost). Celebration symbolism: Mrs. Weasley's satisfied smile after she vaporizes the evil witch Bellatrix Lestrange.

Sideways: Jack and Miles lived the adventure of their lives and succeeded in securing true love. Celebration symbolism: The wedding.

Dodgeball: Average Joe's wins. Everyone cheers and hugs at the stadium.

181 – Atonement

The Hero has made peace with the fatherly figure.

Description:

The Hero has redeemed the father by avenging him or honoring him. More importantly, the Hero transcended the father.

According to American philosopher Ken Wilber, such is the nature of evolution: To simultaneously include and transcend the past. The Hero, identified with the father, has also emerged victorious where the father couldn't.

Examples:

Star Wars: Luke eventually becomes a Jedi, like Anakin before him. But he also transcended his father, because Luke never gave in to the temptation of the Dark Side.

The Matrix: Neo rescued his fatherly figure (Morpheus), succeeding where nobody else ever could.

Harry Potter: By the end of the series, Harry avenged and honored his actual father (James), his Mentor (Dumbledore), and the "bravest man he ever knew" (Snape). And of course, he went beyond all of them.

Sideways: In Miles's novel the character of the father is mentioned in self-destructive ways; Miles surpassed that fictional father, because he still had a chance at happiness, and he decided to take it.

Dodgeball: Peter honored Patches's legacy, and even transcended the glory of the legendary couch, reaching the top of the world—well, of the dodgeball world.

Related:

086 – Atonement: First Foreshadow
121 – Atonement: Second Foreshadow

182 – Magic Flight

The Hero flies away. Really. Or at least the Hero ascends somehow.

Description:

Think of this moment as the ascension of Christ to the Heavens: It is a symbol of the Hero transcending the rank of mere mortal.

This stage is a tricky one. People don't go flying around, so it must happen in a way that doesn't ruin the verisimilitude of the story.

Examples:

Star Wars: Luke returns, piloting his X-wing to the Rebel base. He is literally flying.

The Matrix: Neo ascends to the sky, flying like Superman. Yes, he is literally flying.

Harry Potter: Many episodes of the series end with Harry literally flying, either on a broomstick or on some winged creature.

Sideways: Miles takes the stairs up to Maya's house (he "ascends") before knocking on the door. This has to be the subtlest instance of this stage represented in a film, ever.

Dodgeball: The team "ascends" to fame: They are portrayed on the cover of OSQ—*Obscure Sports Quarterly* magazine.

183 – Refusal of the Return
The Hero enjoys the moment.

Description:

The Hero shows some kind of resistance to leaving the scenario of the final triumph.

Examples:

Star Wars: Luke takes a moment in space. He is at ease, eyes closed. He hears Obi-Wan one last time: "Remember, the Force will be with you. Always."

The Matrix: Neo stands relaxed and with an aura made of Matrix code around him. Trinity has to scream to him, "Neo!," so he picks up the phone before the EMP is triggered.

Harry Potter: School is over. At Hogsmeade's train station Hermione says, "Feels strange to be going home, doesn't it?" Harry answers, "I'm not going home. Not really." The train whistles.

Sideways: The trip is over. On the way back home, Jack crashes Miles's car into a tree, and then they drive it into a pit. They are trying to simulate an accident, to justify Jack's broken nose.

Dodgeball: We see Dwight escorted by two beautiful cheerleaders, Peter escorted by Kate and Joyce, Owen kissing Fran, and Jason and Amber together. This is Vegas, baby: Before returning home, a party is in order.

Related:
184 – Guided Return

184 – Guided Return

The Hero needed help to depart; now the Hero needs help to come back.

Description:

The Goddess helps the Hero to get back from the battle.

In some versions of the Hero's Journey this stage is called "Rescue from Without."

Examples:

Star Wars: People in the hangar helps Luke descend from his starfighter. They also unload R2D2, who was destroyed during the battle.

The Matrix: Trinity disconnects Neo from the Matrix. He awakes in the real world, in her arms.

Harry Potter: Off screen, Hermione helps Ron, who was left unconscious during the chess match, and Harry, who was left unconscious after the fight against Quirrell and Voldemort.

Sideways: Miles drives Jack to Christine's home. She and her family, showing concern about Jack's nose wound, welcome him back.

Dodgeball: (Not applicable).

Related:
183 – Refusal of the Return

185 – Consummation of Love
It's kissing time.

Description:

During the climax, things are too chaotic and hectic. The lovers must wait until after the final battle in order to enjoy a little intimacy.

This stage resolves the previous, failed declarations of love. A kiss is usually in order: It is the single, most universal, purest sign of romantic love.

It's better if this moment is romantic, not sexual. Why? Because sex doesn't resolve things; it complicates them. If there's sex at all in your story, it should have happened before this stage.

Examples:

Star Wars: Leia and Han's consummation of love happens off screen. In *The Empire Strikes Back*, they are already fighting with each other. See? Sex complicated things.

The Matrix: Neo is back from the Matrix. He and Trinity kiss in the real world.

Harry Potter: There are no kisses between them, yet, but Ron and Hermione are shown close to each other on a balcony, waiting for Harry to be released from the hospital wing.

Sideways: The wedding is the Union Symbolism, of course. This approach is a bit tired as a resource, but also a classic.

Dodgeball: Kate kisses Peter. And before that, she kisses Joyce. Who's Joyce? She is Kate's girlfriend. Deal with it.

Related:
124 – First Declaration of Love
168 – Second Declaration of Love

186 – Award Ceremony

Victory is symbolized by the presentation of a valuable object.

Description:

The transfer of a physical object—a trophy—serves as a symbol of recognition.

Important: The trophy is *not* the Boon—it is merely a tangible symbol of the Hero's triumph.

Also, note that unlike stage 180 – Celebration, this stage has a ritual component; it's a ceremony, not a spontaneous reaction.

Examples:

Star Wars: Award ceremony at the Great Temple on planet Yavin. Princess Leia presents the heroes with the medals.

The Matrix: (Not applicable).

Harry Potter: House Cup award ceremony. Gryffindor wins the House Cup thanks to Harry, Ron, and Hermione. And Neville, of course.

Sideways: Wedding ceremony. Miles (the best man) hands the rings over to Jack and Christine.

Dodgeball: Award ceremony at the dodgeball arena. The team gets a trophy, a giant check for $50,000, and a treasure box with the five million that Peter won by betting White's bribe.

187 – Ally Is Fine

Some ally we thought dead is still kicking.

Description:

The return of this ally can either happen either in stage 167 – The Cavalry Arrives or now, providing relief to the audience.

Examples:

Star Wars: R2D2 is repaired, and he's emitting all kinds of beeps and noises (see stage 189 – World Repaired).

The Matrix: Tank is alive (see stage 167 – The Cavalry Arrives).

Harry Potter: Ron was hurt and left unconscious during the chess game; now he is totally recovered.

Sideways: Jack's nose is getting better; we see him at the wedding using a smaller band aid.

Dodgeball: Steve was lost, but he comes back changed for the better (he left the pirate delusion behind).

Related:
167 – The Cavalry Arrives
189 – World Repaired

188 – Time Has Passed
The dust of the final battle has settled down.

Description:

We see the Hero fulfilling a new role in the real world. The Hero looks normal again, not like a semi-god as in stage 177 – Apotheosis. But there is clear progress in the Hero's life in comparison to stage 020 – The Hero's Day Job.

Sometimes, the next generation is shown—the Hero's kids. Or at least there is some allusion to the cyclic nature of time.

Examples:

Star Wars: Luke and Han are now generals in the Rebellion, and Leia is the undiscussed leader.

The Matrix: Neo is back in the Matrix. We see people walking by on a sunny day.

Harry Potter: In *The Deathly Hallows,* nineteen years after the Battle of Hogwarts, the protagonists bid their own kids farewell as the new generation boards the Hogwarts Express. We see who married whom.

Sideways: Miles is back in his class. We hear Maya's voice over: "It's turned cold and rainy here lately, but I like winter." (Note that she mentions the cycle of the seasons).

Dodgeball: Peter and friends are back in the gym, recording a television advertisement. Amber is pregnant, and its full of other kids in there.

189 – World Repaired
There is a return to sharing.

Description:

This stage marks a contrast with stage 019 – Selfishness Is on the Rise and shows that the world has returned to a state of improved normality: People are sharing again.

Usually, graduation is used for symbolism, or some other form of sharing (a toast, a meal, a mass, etc.)

Examples:

Star Wars: R2D2 and C3PO look resplendent. Even Chewbacca looks like he took a shower (reparation symbolism).

The Matrix: Neo looks once again like his handsome self. He is now freeing others, like he was freed once. Ironically, the repairing of the world is shown as a failure in the Matrix (the "System Error" message in the final scene).

Harry Potter: Harry awakens in the Hogwarts hospital wing. People have left flowers, cards, and sweets for him (sharing symbolism). Dumbledore takes a bean from a box of Bertie Bott's Every Flavour Beans (meal symbolism). "Alas," he says, "earwax."

Sideways: Maya's message says that she's about to graduate and will soon leave her job as waitress (graduation symbolism).

Dodgeball: Peter is seen handing towels to customers (sharing symbolism), greeting everyone, in a totally renovated Average Joe's Gymnasium (repair symbolism).

Related:
186 – Award Ceremony

190 – A New Home

The Hero finally finds a place to call home.

Description:

After all the transitions, transmogrifications, changes of name, clothes, and places, the Hero finally finds a place (or a family) to belong.

Examples:

Star Wars: Luke, Leia, and Han were left alone in the world, but they found a new family in each other.

The Matrix: Paradoxically, Neo found a home in the Matrix: As he is The One, the Matrix is exactly his element. In fact, he doesn't spend much time in Zion at all. Also, we can say that he found a home in Trinity.

Harry Potter: Despite having to go back to the Dursleys, Harry found in Hogwarts his true home.

Sideways: Miles found Maya, and in the final scene he is headed to her home.

Dodgeball: The friends return to the only place where they feel at home: Average Joe's Gymnasium.

Bonus Example:

"Home" can have different meanings for different heroes. In *The Hurt Locker*, Sergeant James feels at home in the war. In the last scene, we see him walking down a street in Baghdad, headed to disarm yet another explosive, with a huge smile plastered on his face.

191 – Enlightened Self
The Hero becomes who he/she truly is.

Description:

Time has passed. The Hero has achieved a new, mature self.

He controls his powers, his flaw is transcended, and a new, serene aura surrounds him.

This marks a contrast with the "diamond in the rough" the Hero was in stage 005.

Examples:

Star Wars: Luke Skywalker becomes a true Jedi.

The Matrix: Neo becomes a true savior.

Harry Potter: Harry becomes a true wizard.

Sideways: Miles becomes a true lover.

Dodgeball: Peter La Fleur becomes a true leader.

Related:

005 – The Hero's Talent

192 – Freedom to Live

The Hero chooses a future.

Description:

No matter what was achieved during the quest, the Ultimate Boon is always *freedom*. It is the key to individuation, to be oneself, to become who we are supposed to become.

What will the Hero choose to do when the world has no more impending demands? Well, he usually uses this freedom to continue doing what he does best.

Examples:

Star Wars: Luke chooses to continue fighting for the Rebellion. He becomes a general and a Jedi.

The Matrix: Neo chooses to continue fighting for humanity. He awakes others.

Harry Potter: Harry chooses to continue fighting against evil. He becomes an Auror.

Sideways: Miles continues being a teacher and a writer.

Dodgeball: Peter chooses to continue managing Average Joe's Gym.

193 – Final Bows
The curtain is about to fall.

Description:

Just before the end, many stories recount the destiny of the main characters. It's like at the end of a theater play, when the actors come to the stage to salute and thank the audience.

This farewell rounds the story up by returning to the place where the adventure started. It closes a cycle and reminds the audience how good a time they had.

Examples:

Star Wars: Luke, Leia, Han, Chewbacca, C3PO, and R2D2 stand together in front of the applauding crowd, just like at the end of a theater performance.

The Matrix: We see the surviving heroes back in the Nebuchadnezzar: Neo, Trinity, Morpheus, and Tank. And we see the Matrix, too, in the form of that green computer screen.

Harry Potter: Dumbledore names the kids one by one as he awards last-minute points: Harry, Hermione, Ron, and Neville. We see the rest of the characters as they react to the speech. Everyone is there.

Sideways: We hear Maya's voice in the loving message she leaves in Miles answering machine. Miles is like pinot, and she is graduating as a wine grower—a symbolism that goes back to the central dialogue of the film, back in stage 120.

Dodgeball: The friends are back in the gym. There is a painting of Patches O'Houlihan hanging on a wall. The movie started with a TV spot for Globo Gym, and it ends with a TV spot for Average Joe's.

194 – The Open End
Some element of the dark side remains.

Description:

If your story will have an open end (i.e., evil might return), the challenge lies in making it subtle.

This is easier to pull off in a movie than in a novel, because, how do you write an open end without diluting the satisfaction that the novel's end must provide? That is what we writers have to figure out.

Examples:

Star Wars: Darth Vader is shown regaining control of his fighter. He will be back for another seven films (and counting).

The Matrix: Even when there is a new sheriff in town, the Matrix persists. The fight continues.

Harry Potter: At the end of *The Sorcerer's Stone*, things are just starting. Voldemort survived, of course, to battle it out in seven more movies.

Sideways: The end of this movie mirrors the uncertain ending of Miles's novel. We see him knocking at Maya's door, but we don't see anything else. What happens after that is a mystery. Talk about subtlety.

Dodgeball: In the post-credits sequence, White Goodman, obese and abandoned to excess, sings a rap while holding a piece of fried chicken in his hand. (Is he going to come back? Nah.)

195 – The Actual End

Your story arrives at the last paragraph, the last sentence, and the last word.

Description:

Before writing the last paragraph, go read some poetry. Get inspired. Avoid corniness at all costs, but end with emotion. The end of the book will immensely influence the reader's final opinion about it. Make it memorable.

Examples:

Star Wars: The last "words" are left to R2D2 and Chewbacca: Beeps and growls. We don't know what they mean, but we know they are joyous. Brilliant.

The Matrix: Neo looks at the camera and thanks the audience with the subtlest of smiles. He puts his signature sunglasses on and flies away.

Harry Potter: Harry's son is worried that he might get put into Slytherin house. Harry reminds him that he was named Albus Severus Potter after two Headmasters of Hogwarts; one of them was a Slytherin, and the bravest man Harry knew. And the very last word of the whole story is "Ready." I doubt there is a word that better represents Harry's own bravery.

Sideways: Maya's message ends, "Anyway, like I said, I really loved your novel. Don't give up, Miles. Keep writing."

Dodgeball: The greatest final words in a comedy, ever: "Fucking Chuck Norris!"

Farewell

We arrive at our own *dénouement*, too.

I'm writing these words with a smile and a bit of sadness, because finishing a book (either writing or reading it) is a bittersweet moment. We too resist going back to the Ordinary World—just like the heroes we followed along these pages did.

But hey, this is our guided return: Let's go back to reading great novels and watching great movies. Let's enjoy those beautiful stories, this time with a deeper understanding of what makes them tick.

And remember: I tried my best, but "Nobody can advise you and help you—nobody," Rilke said a century ago in his *Letters to a Young Poet*. "There is only one way. Go into yourself."

So this is my Call to Adventure to you, young Padawan: With a laptop for your lightsaber and black coffee as your Elixir, go find inspiration and write, if that what's you are meant to do. Let your fantasy take off, rising on its own Magic Flight.

Thanks for reading my book. Now it is time to face our dragons and go and write some more.

I believe in you.

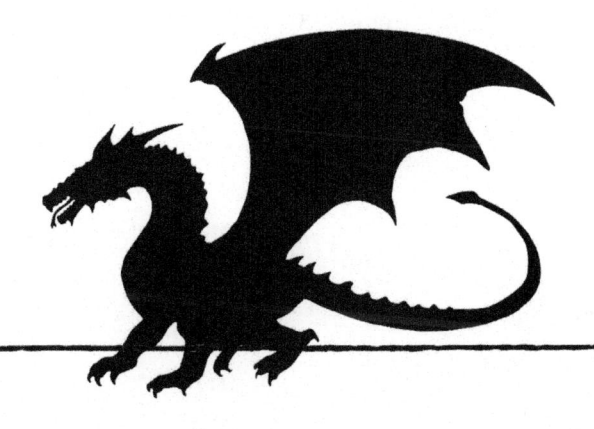

Index of stages

(Remember: the page number is always the same as the stage number. Also, I include Campbell's classic stages in here, so you can relate the sequence to the graphic in the first page of this book.)

Act 1 – Setup

Hook
001 – The Hook

Inciting Event
002 – The Villain
003 – The (Sleeping) Hero
004 – The Hero's Anonymity
005 – The Hero's Talent
006 – Foreshadows
007 – The Surrogate Parents
008 – It's A Hard-Knock Life
009 – Mutual Creation
010 – The Sign Of The One
011 – The Hero's Immaturity
012 – The Hero's Ignorance
013 – The Mentor Awaits
014 – The World In Decadence
015 – Cheating To Get By
016 – The Mentor's Knowledge
017 – Denial Of The Premise
018 – Attack 1: Insult
019 – Selfishness Is On The Rise
020 – The Hero's Day Job
021 – Stuck In The Ordinary World
022 – The Hero's Goal
023 – The Hero's Desire
024 – A Warning And A Threat
025 – The Hero's Ghost
026 – The Hero's Weakness
027 – The Lie the Hero Believes In
028 – Attack 2: Physical Damage
029 – Inciting Event

Index of stages

030 – The Goddess
031 – A Storm Is Coming
032 – Resistance to the Separation
033 – Attack 3: The Hero Resists
034 – The Mentor's Faith
035 – The Villain's Dominion
036 – The Villain's Orders
037 – Secret Message
038 – The Herald
039 – Unusual Places
040 – The Herald Returns

Call To Adventure

041 – Test Of Worthiness
042 – The Herald Guides The Hero
043 – The Hero Is A Mess
044 – Transmogrifications
045 – The Herald's Gift
046 – The Mentor
047 – Quick Introductions
048 – Historical Battle
049 – The Prophecy is Shared
050 – The Prophecy Is Incomplete
051 – Be Careful With What You Wish
052 – Call To Adventure

Refusal of the Call

053 – First Refusal Of The Call
054 – Our Most Desperate Hour
055 – The Mentor's Rebuttal
056 – Presentation of the Sword
057 – Second Refusal Of The Call
058 – The Mentor's Warning
059 – Pushing Event
060 – No Appeal Possible
061 – First Epiphany

Answer To The Call

062 – Answer To The Call

Act 2.1 – Reaction

Crossing The Threshold

063 – The Hero Is Welcome
064 – Plan A: Let Events Unfold
065 – New Clothes
066 – Transitions
067 – The Team Is Assembled
068 – Guardians
069 – Presentation Of The Elixir
070 – Baptism Of Water

Belly Of The Whale

071 – Down The Rabbit Hole
072 – No Going Back
073 – The Hero's Determination
074 – The Traitor
075 – Book Of Laws

Meeting With The Goddess

076 – Encounter With The Goddess
077 – Girl Tests Boy

Index of stages

Road Of Trials

078 – Training: Success
079 – First Encouragement
080 – Training: Failure
081 – The False Enemy
082 – Stakes Increase
083 – The Random Ally
084 – Snake Symbolism
085 – Surpassing Peers
086 – Atonement: First Foreshadow
087 – World Under Surveillance
088 – Good Guys in Disagreement
089 – A Bad Feeling About This
090 – Blindness Symbolism
091 – Attack 4: Interrogation
092 – Attack 5: Spying
093 – Baptism Of Fire: Failure
094 – Baptism Of Fire: Rescue
095 – Attack 6: Intimidation
096 – The Hero Is Recognized
097 – Right Words At The Right Time (1)
098 – The Awkward Innocent
099 – The Lieutenants' Ineptitude
100 – Presentation of Gifts
101 – The Temptress
102 – Attack 7: False Enemy
103 – Maternal Love
104 – The Hero's Improvement
105 – The Villain's Disturbance
106 – A Well Complemented Team
107 – Breaking The Law
108 – People Take Sides
109 – Praise To The Great Mentor
110 – Run for your life (1)
111 – Traitor On The Move
112 – The Villain's True Face
113 – Attack 8: Shock And Awe
114 – The Mentor's Orders
115 – The Mentor's Fight
116 – The Mentor Is Gone
117 – A Moment Of Reflection
118 – The Ultimate Boon

Act 2.2 – Midpoint

Epiphany

119 – Second Epiphany

Act 2.3 – Proaction

Ordeal

120 – Plan B: Rescue
121 – Atonement: Second Foreshadow
122 – The Hero Leads
123 – Run For Your Life (2)
124 – First Declaration Of Love
125 – The Über-Villain
126 – The Villain's Stronghold

127 – A Suicide Mission
128 – The Villain's Speech
129 – The Villain's Shadow
130 – Resentment With The Mentor
131 – The Price Of Victory
132 – Attack 9: The Hero's Lair
133 – Detachment To Protect Allies
134 – The Team Gets Scattered
135 – The Hero's Fall
136 – The Villain Rises
137 – Recrimination By Ally
138 – No Way Back, No Way Forward
139 – Ticking Clock
140 – The Villain's Weakness
141 – Second Encouragement
142 – Third Epiphany

Act 3 – Climax

Final Battle

143 – Plan C: Infiltrate
144 – The Reluctant Aid
145 – The Comedic Relief
146 – Sword Upgrade
147 – Suit Up and Go
148 – Rallying The Troops
149 – Grand Entrance Of The Villain
150 – Humble Entrance Of The Hero
151 – The Villain's Monologue
152 – Temptation Rejected
153 – Back To The Hook
154 – Battle Against Major Guardians
155 – Attack 10: Furious Chase
156 – Battling Styles
157 – Allies Out Of Combat
158 – Run for your life (3)
159 – The Oblivious Innocent
160 – A Cross of Swords
161 – At The Mercy Of The Villain
162 – Death Foretold
163 – The Hero's Death
164 – The Unthinkable Happens
165 – Emergence Of The Elixir
166 – The Hero's Resurrection
167 – The Cavalry Arrives
168 – Second Declaration Of Love
169 – Third Encouragement
170 – Right Words At The Right Time (2)

Apotheosis

171 – The Hero Lets Go
172 – The Hero's Verbal Attack
173 – Emergence Of The Sword
174 – The Hero Is Unstoppable
175 – The Villain "Dies"
176 – Resurrection Of The Villain
177 – Apotheosis

Index of stages

The Ultimate Boon
178 – Lieutenants Vanish

179 – Master Of Two Worlds

180 – Celebration

Atonement
181 – Atonement

Magic Flight
182 – Magic Flight

Return
183 – Refusal Of The Return

184 – Guided Return

185 – Consummation of Love

Act 4 – Dénouement
186 – Award Ceremony

187 – Ally Is Fine

Freedom To Live
188 – Time Has Passed

189 – World Repaired

190 – A New Home

191 – Enlightened Self

192 – Freedom To Live

193 – Final Bows

194 – The Open End

195 – The Actual End

Would you leave a good word for this book on Amazon, so other people interested in the Hero's Journey can find it?

Also, if you want to send me an email, you are most welcome: [Neal@tb-books.com.](mailto:Neal@tb-books.com) I read them all and try my best to answer them all, too.

Another book from our press that you may want to check out:

"A fascinating, entertaining, and extremely useful read for the multitalented."
-Robert Shaw, author (www.roberteshaw.com)

THE DA VINCI CURSE

Life design for people with **too many** interests and talents

Leonardo Lospennato

Notes

Notes

Notes

Notes

Notes

Notes

Printed in Great Britain
by Amazon